Celebrity Culture

Lisa Idzikowski, Book Editor

GREENHAVEN
PUBLISHING

Published in 2021 by Greenhaven Publishing, LLC
353 3rd Avenue, Suite 255, New York, NY 10010

First Edition

Articles in Greenhaven Publishing anthologies are often edited for length to meet page requirements. In addition, original titles of these works are changed to clearly present the main thesis and to explicitly indicate the author's opinion. Every effort is made to ensure that Greenhaven Publishing accurately reflects the original intent of the authors. Every effort has been made to trace the owners of the copyrighted material.

Library of Congress Cataloging-in-Publication Data

Names: Idzikowski, Lisa, editor.
Title: Celebrity culture / Lisa Idzikowski, book editor.
Description: First edition. | New York : Greenhaven Publishing, 2021. | Series: Introducing
  issues with opposing viewpoints | Includes bibliographic reference and index. | Audience:
  Grades 7–12.
Identifiers: ISBN 9781534507210 (library binding) | ISBN 9781534507203 (paperback)
Subjects: LCSH: Celebrities—Juvenile literature. | Popular culture—Juvenile literature.
Classification: LCC HM621.C454 2021 | DDC 306—dc23

Manufactured in the United States of America

Website: http://greenhavenpublishing.com

Contents

Chapter 3: Is the Influence of Celebrity Culture on Society Dangerous?

Foreword

Indulging in a wide spectrum of ideas, beliefs, and perspectives is a critical cornerstone of democracy. After all, it is often debates over differences of opinion, such as whether to legalize abortion, how to treat prisoners, or when to enact the death penalty, that shape our society and drive it forward. Such diversity of thought is frequently regarded as the hallmark of a healthy and civilized culture. As the Reverend Clifford Schutjer of the First Congregational Church in Mansfield, Ohio, declared in a 2001 sermon, "Surrounding oneself with only like-minded people, restricting what we listen to or read only to what we find agreeable is irresponsible. Refusing to entertain doubts once we make up our minds is a subtle but deadly form of arrogance." With this advice in mind, Introducing Issues with Opposing Viewpoints books aim to open readers' minds to the critically divergent views that comprise our world's most important debates.

Introducing Issues with Opposing Viewpoints simplifies for students the enormous and often overwhelming mass of material now available via print and electronic media. Collected in every volume is an array of opinions that captures the essence of a particular controversy or topic. Introducing Issues with Opposing Viewpoints books embody the spirit of nineteenth-century journalist Charles A. Dana's axiom: "Fight for your opinions, but do not believe that they contain the whole truth, or the only truth." Absorbing such contrasting opinions teaches students to analyze the strength of an argument and compare it to its opposition. From this process readers can inform and strengthen their own opinions, or be exposed to new information that will change their minds. Introducing Issues with Opposing Viewpoints is a mosaic of different voices. The authors are statesmen, pundits, academics, journalists, corporations, and ordinary people who have felt compelled to share their experiences and ideas in a public forum. Their words have been collected from newspapers, journals, books, speeches, interviews, and the Internet, the fastest growing body of opinionated material in the world.

Introducing Issues with Opposing Viewpoints shares many of the well-known features of its critically acclaimed parent series, Opposing

Viewpoints. The articles allow readers to absorb and compare divergent perspectives. Active reading questions preface each viewpoint, requiring the student to approach the material thoughtfully and carefully. Photographs, charts, and graphs supplement each article. A thorough introduction provides readers with crucial background on an issue. An annotated bibliography points the reader toward articles, books, and websites that contain additional information on the topic. An appendix of organizations to contact contains a wide variety of charities, nonprofit organizations, political groups, and private enterprises that each hold a position on the issue at hand. Finally, a comprehensive index allows readers to locate content quickly and efficiently.

Introducing Issues with Opposing Viewpoints is also significantly different from Opposing Viewpoints. As the series title implies, its presentation will help introduce students to the concept of opposing viewpoints and learn to use this material to aid in critical writing and debate. The series' four-color, accessible format makes the books attractive and inviting to readers of all levels. In addition, each viewpoint has been carefully edited to maximize a reader's understanding of the content. Short but thorough viewpoints capture the essence of an argument. A substantial, thought-provoking essay question placed at the end of each viewpoint asks the student to further investigate the issues raised in the viewpoint, compare and contrast two authors' arguments, or consider how one might go about forming an opinion on the topic at hand. Each viewpoint contains sidebars that include at-a-glance information and handy statistics. A Facts About section located in the back of the book further supplies students with relevant facts and figures.

Following in the tradition of the Opposing Viewpoints series, Greenhaven Publishing continues to provide readers with invaluable exposure to the controversial issues that shape our world. As John Stuart Mill once wrote: "The only way in which a human being can make some approach to knowing the whole of a subject is by hearing what can be said about it by persons of every variety of opinion and studying all modes in which it can be looked at by every character of mind. No wise man ever acquired his wisdom in any mode but this." It is to this principle that Introducing Issues with Opposing Viewpoints books are dedicated.

Introduction

"Where once the famous achieved an almost godlike status, one that seemed impermeable and historical (consider Lincoln or Washington, Charles Lindbergh or Jesse Owens), today celebrity exists for and by an information age. In our global and atomized world of bits and bytes, where information is instantly available and massive in its quantities, and as perishable as an electronic image, celebrities help personalize that information. They put a human face on it. However, they are diminished in the process. The trouble is, so are we."

—Jill Neimark, "The Culture of Celebrity," *Psychology Today*

Fame, huge houses and estates, jetting around the world, unending heaps of money, fancy clothes, expensive cars and jewelry, servants, chauffeurs, and more. These things most likely come to mind when people think of celebrities and celebrity culture. But how accurate is this? Are these the only things associated with being a celebrity? Is celebrity status always a positive state of being? Are there negative aspects to celebrity?

Celebrities have been around in different forms for a very long time. Egyptians revered their pharaohs. Christians, Jews, and Muslims have looked to Jesus Christ, Yahweh, and Mohammed. George Washington, Queen Victoria, Albert Einstein, Winston Churchill, Franklin D. Roosevelt, Joan of Arc, Charles Darwin, and innumerable others have been important figures throughout history, and arguably famous. But, probably without much disagreement, people today view celebrities and celebrity culture mostly as movie stars, sports figures, music icons, politicians, social media sensations, and business CEO's. And depending upon a person's age, their universe of celebrities looks very different—Taylor Swift, Drake, Elvis Presley, The Beatles, The Kardashians, Joe Namath, Serena Williams, Brett Favre, Pele, Morgan Freeman, Bill Gates, Angelina Jolie,

Denzel Washington, Michael Jackson, Beyoncé, Katharine Hepburn, Michael Jordan, and countless others have been celebrities at one time or another.

Clearly there are upsides and downsides to the whole issue of celebrity. Many people would say that money and wealth are a big deal. According to Pew Research, 20 percent of all adults under 30 years of age agree that being wealthy is a top priority. And yes, there are fantastically wealthy celebrities spending loads of money to maintain a celebrity culture lifestyle. But surprisingly the rich can fall into financial problems just like the average public. Michael Jackson was at least $400 million in debt when he unexpectedly died in 2009, according to Business Insider reporting.

Of course, not all celebrities are mired in selfishness and money worship. There are many out there dedicating a portion of their lives for good causes. Chance the Rapper supports public schools in Chicago, Taylor Swift speaks out against sexual harassment, Leonardo DiCaprio works for environmental causes, and Bill Gates gives to Alzheimer's research, among others. Besides this, how many of us would like to be hounded by the press, photographers fans, and critics? Celebrities often complain that this is unacceptable. England's Prince Harry has often commented how he believes the unrelenting paparazzi had a hand in the ultimate death of his mother, Princess Diana.

Celebrity culture has changed through time. Some experts point to the development of media technologies as a reason for this change. Just think how the world has changed with the coming of the internet and social media. Examples are everywhere of the effects of Facebook, Twitter, Instagram, and other media. Lots of young people want nothing more than to be famous. *Teen Vogue* reported that 31 percent of teens not only want to be famous, but actually think they may achieve celebrity status. This does not bode well for society, in which fulfilling jobs are necessary to make communities run. What happened to youth wanting to become nurses, teachers, or firefighters?

Does this mean that celebrities and celebrity culture are a dangerous influence in society? Not necessarily. Certainly, celebrities do have an impact beyond entertainment.

In 1960, presidential candidate John F. Kennedy had the support of Rat Pack members (entertainers loved by the public of that time period) Sammy Davis Jr and Dean Martin. More recently, research done by the University of Maryland shows that Oprah Winfrey helped Barack Obama receive more than a million votes in the 2008 presidential race because she supported his candidacy. Years later in 2016, Taylor Swift encouraged voting, and consequently, voter registrations among young people aged 18 to 24 jumped substantially.

This fascination with celebrities and celebrity culture also promotes differing health outcomes, both good and bad. Psychologist Abby Aronowitz has found that idolizing "someone for their accomplishments can spur you on to make gains in your own life," which can have a positive influence on mental health. Experts at *Psychology Today* found that people who look to celebrities for entertainment reasons were more optimistic, happy, and outgoing. On the flip side, Eric Hollander, professor of psychiatry at the Mt. Sinai School of Medicine in New York, reports that an increasing number of individuals have a fascination with celebrities, which replaces people's focus on real life—and that can become a major problem for some individuals.

Are people too concerned with celebrity culture? Is this dangerous for society? Are there positive aspects to being tuned in to the rich and famous? The current debate that surrounds this relevant topic is explored in *Introducing Issues with Opposing Viewpoints: Celebrity Culture,* shedding light on this fascinating and ongoing contemporary issue.

Chapter 1

Why Are We Fascinated by Celebrity?

Is there anyone who doesn't dream of being important enough to sail past the velvet rope?

Viewpoint

1

Is It Always Good to Be a Famous Celebrity?

"You may be thinking a celebrity has everything in life, but there are several downsides of being famous."

Ella Maclin

In the following viewpoint Ella Maclin argues that most people see celebrity status as a living style to achieve. The author analyzes the advantages and the disadvantages of celebrity. A possibly surprising fact that Maclin puts forth is that some celebrities deal with depression and sometimes are driven to commit suicide. Ella Maclin is a blogger and content writer at the Healthy Suggestions.

AS YOU READ, CONSIDER THE FOLLOWING QUESTIONS:

1. According to the author, what is a universal belief about celebrity that may be wrong?
2. According to the viewpoint, what are two advantages of being a celebrity?
3. What are two disadvantages of celebrity, according to the author?

Popularity is something most of us dream of. Think about those luxury cars, mansions, lots of money, and millions of fans shouting your name. Only getting engaged in the show-biz world will help us achieve those material things and live a lavish life in an instant.

However, is it worth it? Is being famous good all the time?

The deaths of celebrities like Michael Jackson left us a question mark whether or not they were able to live the life they truly wanted. On the other hand, the eternal fame of various celebrities these days still give us a puzzling answer whether they are really happy being in the international scene or not. Especially now, the number of personalities who commit suicide due to depression is alarming.

Being a Celebrity Means Dealing with Various Ups and Downs

Who said being popular is always fun?

Being famous has its advantages and disadvantages. You may be thinking a famous personality or celebrity has everything in life (a universal insight of people), but in reality, there are also several disadvantages and downsides of being famous.

Perks of Being a Celebrity

Being Richer

Obviously the greatest advantage of being a celebrity. Generally, fame brings a lot of fortune. They live in beautiful mansions or houses maintained by gardeners, cook, housekeepers, and other servants.

Also, they can afford to buy the best clothes and everything they want, don't need to worry about paying bills, drive the newest car models, travel a lot, buy fancy gifts, spend their vacations or holidays in the most luxurious resorts, and so much more! Celebrities are usually more luxurious than the average Joe.

Recognized Locally and Globally

Famous personalities are recognized wherever they go. This is a great ego boost. Besides, they can meet other celebrities and are invited to the best parties.

Being swarmed by fans and photographers comes with the territory for megacelebrities like Justin Bieber.

Various Opportunities

Many different opportunities arise when a person becomes famous. For instance, Kim Kardashian is not only renowned in the entertainment industry but manages to wedge in newer businesses such as perfumes and apparel. Starting businesss is what most celebrities choose once they reach stardom.

Have Supportive Fans

Isn't it very overwhelming to know there are millions of people out there who are willing to share your happiness and sadness? After all, a celebrity would not be able to reach the success he or she is gaining without these ever-supportive fans.

Fan mail and any other forms of appreciation that a popular personality receive can be very humbling, motivational, and inspirational. Everyone likes to have their followers, worshippers, and fans.

Get Special Treatment Everywhere They Go

Be that special tables at restaurants, special seats at theaters, or others, celebrities are given the perks of being the most favorite customers wherever they go. Surely, you would also love getting the first row seats at a special event or having preferred entry at nightclubs.

These are the perks that a celebrity could get out of being famous. And who wouldn't want to experience these?

The Downsides of Being a Celebrity
No Privacy
Whether you like it or not, every detail about yourself, your family or love life will be the talk of the town. As soon as you enter showbiz, you need to accept that your life is not just yours anymore—it is everyone's.

Paparazzi
Even if is just about getting a cup of coffee nearby or going to a supermarket, expect a group of people to mob and hound you for pictures and autographs.

Stalker
Stalkers can be a real headache when you become a celebrity. You probably know about the stalkers of Whitney Houston, one of them was sending her flowers, calling her offices, and worst, harassing her. Hence, being popular means watching your back … ALWAYS.

Rumors. Rumors. Rumors.
People love starting rumors about celebs. It may not be a big deal sometimes, but in most cases, people can say some foul things about you. This can eventually have a negative impact on your life, your family, or your future. The worst rumor can be about someone's death! It was at the beginning of this year a series of posts reported Sylvester Stallone death from cancer. Fortunately, it was just an internet hoax but it definitely hurt him, people, who are close to him and even his fans.

Never-ending Travel
If you're a type of person who doesn't love traveling a lot, then becoming celebrity might challenge you. Famous personalities tend to have to be away from family and friends for an extended period.

Trust Issues

In the world of showbiz, you don't really know who your real friends are. You don't know who deserves your trust or who will jeopardize your friendship. You don't even know who can offer you, genuine love. So, it is essential to watch your back and scrutinize each person that comes into your life.

Can't Mess Up

Ever wanted to go "crazy" sometimes but worry that someone might catch you and lose their respect for you? Celebrities surely want to let loose but many choose to maintain a clean image so as not to ruin their reputation and status.

Indeed, it might not be always good to be famous because of these disadvantages. So, would you still choose to be a celebrity?

Final Thoughts

So as you see, being famous is both a gift and awful. You get to appreciate all the material things you have and live a luxurious life as long as you want, but some things need to be set aside, like your privacy. Popularity can make or break you, and it depends upon you on how to make the best use of this once-in-a-lifetime opportunity.

EVALUATING THE AUTHOR'S ARGUMENTS:

In this viewpoint, Ella Maclin presents a balanced view of the advantages and disadvantages of having celebrity status. Construct an argument using Maclin's points and answer the question: Is celebrity status worth it?

Overeager Photographers Put Celebrities at Risk

Kayleigh Dray

"The paparazzi consistently go to increasingly dangerous lengths to stalk and harass the people they are photographing."

In the following viewpoint Kayleigh Dray analyzes the issue of how celebrities are chased and harassed by the paparazzi. Specifically, Dray draws on incidents from the lives of American actress Scarlett Johansson and Britain's Princess Diana to highlight the issue of danger that this paparazzi attention causes for people in the public eye. Kayleigh Dray is an editor with Stylist.com.uk, where she writes about television, films, comic books, and feminism.

AS YOU READ, CONSIDER THE FOLLOWING QUESTIONS:
1. How should paparazzi be "classified" according to Scarlett Johansson?
2. What makes the paparazzi so dangerous according to Johansson?
3. According to the author, how should the paparazzi have helped Princess Diana?

Earlier this week, Scarlett Johansson was spotted by a group of photographers as she left the Jimmy Kimmel Live! studios in Los Angeles. The *Avengers: Endgame* actress alleges that the paparazzi, in a bid to find out where she and her child were staying, jumped into five cars with blacked-out windows and chased her across the city, running red lights in their desperation and putting "other drivers and pedestrians ... at risk" in order to get the shots they wanted.

"The paparazzi consistently go to increasingly dangerous lengths to stalk and harass the people they are photographing," she said via an official statement. "Even after Princess Diana's tragic death, the laws were never changed to protect targets from the lawless paparazzi.

"Many paparazzi have criminal pasts and will perform criminal acts to get their shot."

The actress went on to note that "it was my duty as a concerned citizen" to notify police of the incident, and has called for changes to the law for paparazzi, insisting they be classified as "criminal stalkers."

"Women across the US are stalked, harassed and frightened and a universal law to address stalking must be at the forefront of law enforcement conversations," she said.

"Until paparazzi are considered by the law for the criminal stalkers they are, it's just a waiting game before another person gets seriously injured or killed, like Princess Diana."

In 2017, Prince Harry and his brother, Prince William, emotionally discussed the events surrounding the car crash that killed their mother, Princess Diana.

Speaking in *Diana: 7 Days*, a new BBC documentary, Harry recalled the moment he first found out that his mother had passed away—and praised his father, Prince Charles, for the way he supported him and his brother through their grief.

"One of the hardest things for a parent to have to do is to tell your children that your other parent has died," he said.

> **FAST FACT**
>
> In 2008, a British jury ruled that both the paparazzi and driver were the cause of the car crash that killed Britain's Princess Diana.

Tabloid photographers earn their living following celebrities and selling photographs of them. Many celebrities consider this stalking.

"How you deal with that I don't know but, you know, he was there for us. He was the one, out of two, left and he tried to do his best and to make sure we were protected and looked after. But, you know, he was going through the same grieving process as well."

When it came to the subject of the world's press, though, Harry admitted that their lack of respect left him and his brother furious.

"I think one of the hardest things to come to terms with is the fact that the people that chased her through into the tunnel were the same people that were taking photographs of her, while she was still dying on the back seat of the car," recalled the prince.

"William and I know that, we've been told that numerous times by people that know that was the case.

"She'd had a … quite a severe head injury, but she was very much still alive on the back seat, and those people that … that caused the accident, instead of helping, were taking photographs of her dying on the back seat.

"And then those photographs made … made their way back to news desks in this country."

Harry and his brother went on to defend the Queen's decision to remain at Balmoral with them rather than return to London—an act which she was criticized for, as members of the public felt that she should support them instead.

Harry and William (aged 15 and 12 at the time) soon found themselves overwhelmed by the public show of grief; returning to London proved to be an utterly bewildering and—at times—frightening experience for them.

"They were grabbing us and pulling us into their arms and stuff," revealed Harry. "I don't blame anyone for that, of course I don't. But it was those moments that were quite shocking.

"People were screaming, people were crying, people's hands were wet because of the tears they had just wiped away from their faces before shaking my hand.

"It was so unusual for people to see young boys like that not crying when everybody else was crying. What we were doing was being asked of us was verging on normal then, but now…"

He pauses, before adding: "Looking at us then, we must have been in just this state of shock."

EVALUATING THE AUTHOR'S ARGUMENTS:

In this viewpoint author Kayleigh Dray makes an argument for reigning in the capabilities of the paparazzi. Should celebrities have to endure harassment by photographers since they are public figures? Use facts from the viewpoint to support your opinion.

Celebrities Can Use Their Fame to Be Agents of Change

"Many recognize that with great social power comes great responsibility and act accordingly to influence the world in positive ways."

Sara Barnes

In the following viewpoint Sara Barnes maintains that some celebrities are actually doing good for others instead of vainly spending their fortunes on themselves. The author examines the charity actions of ten different celebrities, most from the entertainment industry and one a prominent tech sector guru, that give their time and financial support to different social and environmental causes. Sara Barnes is a freelance writer.

AS YOU READ, CONSIDER THE FOLLOWING QUESTIONS:
1. According to the author, which three musical celebrities support agendas of good or change?
2. Which late night TV host promotes health care issues as reported by the viewpoint?
3. Who is the tech giant that supports health research according to the author?

Not all celebrities are galavanting around town and spending all of their money on fancy cars and jewelry. Many recognize that with great social power comes great responsibility, and act accordingly to influence the world in positive ways. From healthcare to the environment, here are 10 celebrities who are using their influence to do good in the world.

1. Chance the Rapper & Chicago Schools

When school budgets get slashed, art funding is often the first to go. Chance the Rapper is helping ensure that Chicago Public Schools have a strong curriculum, especially for inner-city kids. "Quality education for public schools is the most important investment a community can make," he said in a speech. Over the next three years, 20 schools will receive $100,000—a total of $2.2 million raised by his nonprofit.

2. Shailene Woodley & Dakota Pipeline

In 2016, Shailene Woodley joined the group fighting the Dakota Access Pipeline and used her celebrity to raise awareness about the crisis facing the Native Americans as well as the environment itself. Woodley was arrested on October 10, 2016 for criminal trespassing and engaging in a riot. In a response, published on *Time*, she writes, "We grow up romanticizing native culture, native art, native history … without knowing native reality." Later in the essay, she urges, "The Dakota Access Pipeline, my friends, is not another time to ignore, mistreat and turn a blind eye to Native Americans."

3. Ashton Kutcher & Anti-Sex Trafficking

Ashton Kutcher is working to combat modern slavery. In 2009, he and his then-wife Demi Moore founded Thorn: Digital Defenders of Children that engineers "software to fight human trafficking."

Actress Jane Fonda has been an outspoken activist throughout her career, most recently supporting environmental causes.

Calling Thorn his "day job", he testified before the Senate Foreign Relations Committee on trafficking. Of one of their tools, Spotlight, he explains, "In six months, with 25% of our users reporting, we've identified over 6,000 trafficking victims, 2,000 of which are minors. This tool has enhanced 4,000 law enforcement officials in 900 agencies. And we're reducing the investigation time by 60%."

4. Lily Allen & Syrian Refugees

Lily Allen is not staying silent when it comes to the Syrian refugee crisis. In 2016, she traveled to the Calais in France, a migrant camp. "I went to Calais because I wanted to do what I can to help," she writes. "I wanted to try to remind people of the humanity at the heart of the crisis, at a time when refugees were being demonized in the press."

5. Leonardo DiCaprio & the Environment

Leonardo DiCaprio is known for always having a model on his arm, but beyond his social life and films, he's on a mission to help save

Earth. The Leonardo DiCaprio Foundation is "dedicated to the long-term health and well-being of all Earth's inhabitants." Through grant-making partnerships, they are focused on protecting wildlife from extinction and restoring balance to ecosystems and communities threatened by climate change. Another strong advocate of the environment is singer Pharrell, who even took his fight to the United Nations a few years back surrounded by a thousand middle schoolers. "We only have one home. If you don't take care of your home, you don't have a life. We have to transition from climate change to climate action," he said.

6. Jimmy Kimmel & US Healthcare

When Obamacare was on the chopping block in 2017, there was an unlikely (and unofficial) spokesperson for it: Jimmy Kimmel. On his late-night TV show, he repeatedly called out senators whose legislation and opinions hurt everyone's access to healthcare; at one point, Kimmel got very personal and gave an emotional account of his son's "terrifying" heart defect and surgery. During the monologue, he said, "If your baby is going to die and it doesn't have to, it shouldn't matter how much money you make," he added. "I think that's something that whether you're a Republican or a Democrat or something else, we all agree on that, right?"

7. Taylor Swift & Sexual Harassment

In 2013, Taylor Swift was posing with fans during a pre-concert photo opportunity when an ex-DJ named David Mueller grabbed her bottom. After Swift's team reported the incident to the radio station, the DJ lost his job—and filed a defamation lawsuit against the singer. Swift filed a countersuit and during her bold testimony in court, won the case against Mueller. During her testimony, which was described as "sharp, gutsy, and satisfying," she showed her young fans and other women that you can stand up to sexual assault. "I acknowledge the privilege that I benefit from in life, in society and in my ability to shoulder the enormous cost of defending myself in a trial like this," she said in a statement. "My hope is to help those whose voices should also be heard."

8. Bruno Mars & Flint Water Crisis

The water crisis in Flint, Michigan, will have ripple affects for years to come. During a concert in Auburn Hills, Michigan, the singer revealed that he donated $1 million to aid the victims of this crisis. "Ongoing challenges remain years later for Flint residents, and it's important that we don't forget our brothers and sisters affected by this disaster," he said in a statement. "As people, especially as Americans, we need to stand together to make sure something like this never happens in any community ever again."

9. Bill Gates & Alzheimer's Research

Alzheimer's is a devastating disease—the sixth leading cause of death in the United States—for which there is no treatment nor way to slow its progression. Microsoft co-founder Bill Gates is on a mission to find a cure. He has several family members who have had the disease. "That's not my sole motivation, but it certainly drew me in," he told CNN. He's spent over the past year investigating and talking to scientists to determine how to best help them towards a treatment of Alzheimer's. "I'm a huge believer in that science and innovation are going to solve most of the tough problems over time," he said.

10. Stephen Colbert & Puerto Rico Recovery

In the fall of 2017, celebrities started sharing awkward pictures of their younger selves with the hashtag #PuberMe. The challenge was launched by Stephen Colbert and Nick Kroll, and it spurred donations to Puerto Rico relief. For every celebrity who Instagrammed and/or tweeted the photo and hashtag, Colbert's AmeriCone Dream Fund donated $1,000 to One America Appeal, an organization started by the five living former American Presidents setup to support recovery efforts from Hurricane Harvey, Irma, and Maria.

EVALUATING THE AUTHOR'S ARGUMENTS:

In this viewpoint Sara Barnes analyzes the actions of ten different celebrities that use their notoriety and personal finances to support special causes that benefit society. Are any of your celebrity favorites on this list? Do you know if your favorite celebrities promote social causes? Does it make a difference to you whether your favorite celebrity shows that they care for others?

Viewpoint
4

Celebrity Should Not Be Confused with Expertise

Steven Novella

"We need to be vigilant about surrendering our thinking to others."

In the following viewpoint Steven Novella explains how elevating celebrities to a pedestal of knowledge is a dangerous situation. Novella has no disagreement with celebrities being experts at their craft of entertainment, but when they pretend to be knowledgeable in areas outside their wheelhouse, say in science, that's when he gets worried. Novella maintains that the public is ignoring real knowledge from true experts, instead listening to celebrities capitalizing on their notoriety. Steven Novella is president of the New England Skeptical Society and writes a blog covering issues concerned with science, skepticism, critical thinking, and neuroscience.

AS YOU READ, CONSIDER THE FOLLOWING QUESTIONS:
1. What is Novella's chief disagreement with actress Zooey Deschanel?
2. According to the author what is the difference between celebrities and true experts?
3. What advice does Novella give to the public about authority?

"The Dangers of Celebrity Culture," by Steven Novella, NeuroLogica Blog, January 18, 2018. Reprinted by permission.

Zooey Deschanel has a Facebook page where she gives advice on complex scientific topics. I love Deschanel as an actress and enjoy much of her work (particularly the otherwise mediocre movie version of the Hitchhiker's Guide), but that does not mean I want to take advice from her on which foods I should eat.

Celebrity culture, in one form or another, has always been part of human society. Even chimpanzees will follow a charismatic leader, and it seems likely that humans are wired also to follow those we admire, and elevate them perhaps a bit too much. There is even research that shows that when we listen to a charismatic speaker the executive function part of our frontal lobes shuts down. We literally turn off our critical thinking when basking in the glow of our glorious leader.

Recognizing that this is part of the human condition is important. First, we need to be vigilant about surrendering our thinking to others. It's also important to remind ourselves that everyone is a flawed human, and so constantly give those pedestals a reality check.

But that does not mean we should not admire and respect those who deserve it, or even look up to them for wisdom (as long as we maintain our critical eye). It does mean we need to choose carefully those we respect and follow.

Many people have written recently about the death of expertise. This is a concerning trend of lessening respect for those with genuine expertise, earned through years of study and experience, and often evaluated in some formal way. This may just be a historical trend swinging back and forth, and we happen to be going through a period of populist rejection of authority. Regardless of cause, it is a dangerous trend. We live in an extremely complex technological civilization. Our lives literally depend on countless experts doing jobs we do not understand (or may not even know that they exist). It's hard to know exactly how fragile the whole system is, but I don't really want to find out.

But here is another point—while populists congratulate themselves for being independent thinkers and rejecting the authority of experts, they aren't really. They are just replacing one set of authority figures for another. In many cases celebrity culture is stepping in to fill the void, and the result is not likely to be good.

Gwyneth Paltrow is a respected and award-winning actress. But she has taken heat for the pseudoscience pushed by her wellness company, Goop.

In a recent commentary on the phenomenon, Michael Schulson points out:

As many celebrities have discovered, the combination of wellness culture, ethical consumerism, and Hollywood glamor can make for a potent—and profitable—media cocktail. Pioneers of the model include Gwyneth Paltrow's Goop, a health and lifestyle brand, Jessica Alba's Honest Company, and even Tom Brady's TB12.

Exactly. I would add that sometimes health gurus become celebrities (Dr. Oz), and sometimes celebrities become health gurus, but the end result is usually the same. Paltrow's Goop is probably the most successful example at this point, but there have been and will be others.

The very fact that Oprah's name was seriously floated as a potential presidential candidate indicates how pervasive celebrity culture is. (I have already dealt with this nonsense.)

Spend any amount of time having discussions with those who follow any anti-science echochamber, an ideological belief, or a celebrity guru and you will see that they simultaneously rail against bowing to the authority of academics or scientists, as they are bowing to the authority of their guru or group.

We often make fun of those who claim they have "done their research" because what they really mean is that they have read a bunch of biased and cherry picked articles by hacks dedicated to an anti-scientific agenda.

Getting back to Deschanel—in one of her videos she literally advises people who are too poor to buy all organic to not eat certain vegetables, such as apples, tomatoes, grapes, peppers, and potatoes, because they may contain pesticides. This is a perfect example of how following fear and pseudoscience often leads to the exact opposite of what you want to achieve.

First, there is no evidence that eating fruits and vegetables poses any health risk due to pesticides. Residues are carefully regulated to be far below safety limits. Further, if you want to give yourself even more of a buffer of safety, then just wash your produce thoroughly.

Also, people on a limited budget tend to have worse diets, with real health consequences. Scaring them into avoiding cheap and abundant vegetables is really counterproductive. It also is a manifestation of privileged residents of industrialized nations imposing their nonsense on those with less privilege and causing harm. They have the luxury of wasting money on boutique food to make themselves feel better, but they should stop interfering with those for whom a healthful diet is not a given.

It also has to be pointed out that organic farming can and often does use pesticides. For marketing, they mostly use pesticides they can sell as "natural"—but they are usually more toxic than conventional pesticides, and have to be applied in larger amounts and more often. This is because they are not using the best pesticide, but ones that feel "natural" even if they are worse.

But Deschanel, steeped in Hollywood culture, and without any relevant actual expertise, is now perpetuating these marketing myths based on fear, and is giving bad advice. She is actually telling poor people to avoid certain vegetables in their diet, or waste money they really can't afford on the worthless organic label.

I don't mind if celebrities lend their fame to a cause, or give voice to a science documentary. That's all good. But they should not confuse their celebrity with expertise, or wisdom, or really anything else. More importantly, the public should not make this mistake. I do think it is probably good advice to separate the art from the artists. Famous actors are good at acting, and I will enjoy their art—but I really don't care about their opinions on science or health topics, or even their political opinions. If they want to be taken seriously on a topic other than acting, they will need to earn that right separate from their celebrity.

And in general—maintain a healthy skepticism toward any authority, and choose your authority figures wisely. Specifically, fame and even charisma should probably not even be criteria.

EVALUATING THE AUTHOR'S ARGUMENTS:

In this viewpoint Steven Novella seeks to clarify the distinction of being good as a celebrity in entertainment vs. being an expert in a certain discipline such as science. How do Novella's ideas compare with those of Sara Barnes when she speaks of celebrities doing good in the areas of science?

Celebrity Should Be Used as a Platform for Supporting Good Causes

"Hollywood is budding with actresses, models and celebrities that are also honing in making the world a better place."

Kyla Nwede

In the following viewpoint Kyla Nwede puts a spotlight on five actors, models, and singers that contribute time and finances to social causes. The author maintains that many people think of Angelina Jolie when they want an example of a celebrity that is committed to doing good, but there are many others also making an impact. Kyla Nwede has studied marketing and management for social impact and the public good at Boston College and has spent time volunteering in Chile.

AS YOU READ, CONSIDER THE FOLLOWING QUESTIONS:

1. According to the author, which actor is one of the biggest advocates for LGBTQ issues?
2. Which singer provides support to children in her native country of Colombia?
3. Which actor in the viewpoint article advocates for survivors of sexual assault?

When you think of a humanitarian celebrity, Angelina Jolie usually comes first to mind. Her status as one of the most philanthropic actresses in Hollywood is well-deserved. Jolie serves as an ambassador to the United Nations High Commissioner for Refugees (UNHCR), has fought for the education rights for international children as a co-chair for the Education Partnership for Children of Conflict and has received numerous awards, such as the Citizen of the World Award by the United Nations Correspondents Association.

But if you look beyond Jolie, you'll find that Hollywood is budding with actresses, models and celebrities that are also honing in on making the world a better place.

Here are five women who are also using their fame to stand up and fight for what they believe in.

Laverne Cox

Playing Sophia Burset from Netflix's hit show *Orange Is The New Black*, Laverne Cox is one of the biggest names in LGBTQ advocacy. By just being herself, Laverne Cox proves time and time again that talent is not limited by race, gender or sexuality.

Beyond her role as Sophia, Cox has used her fame to actively discuss and spread awareness of what it means to be both a person of color and a transgender woman. Among many of her accomplishments and awards, Laverne is the first openly transgender woman to be nominated for a Primetime Emmy Award, feature on the cover of TIME and have a wax figure at Madame Tussauds.

She is currently producing a documentary titled *Free Cece* in order to heighten visibility and awareness surrounding CeCe McDonald, a transgender woman convicted of second degree manslaughter "after allegedly defending herself against a racist and transphobic attack," says *Huffington Post*.

Gabrielle Union

You may recognize her from *10 Things I Hate About You* and *Bring It On*. Gabrielle Union has quite the impressive acting resume. Now also known as the star of BET's *Being Mary Jane* and the wife of

Movie star Angelina Jolie has shifted her focus from acting to philanthropy. She has traveled the world as a United Nations ambassador.

NBA Star Dwayne Wade, there is more to this actress than meets the eye.

Gabrielle Union is also an advocate for survivors of sexual assault as she is a survivor herself. Attributing her own survival to the *Oprah Winfrey Show*, Gabrielle uses her own experience and voice to speak out on the issues surrounding sexual assault and rape.

Iman

Iman is one of the most important women in the modeling industry. With 14 years experience as a high fashion model, Iman represented the works of designers such as Gianni Versace, Issey Miyake, Halston, Calvin Klein and Yves Saint-Laurent.

Born and raised in Somalia, Iman shares her experiences as a woman with a dark skin tone. Realizing the limited supply of makeup products available to people of color, Iman turned around created her own cosmetic line with the regal name IMAN. Furthermore, Iman continues to speak out on the lack of diversity in both the fashion and beauty industries.

Shakira

After taking the world by storm with her hit song "Hips Don't Lie," Shakira became Colombia's sweetheart. With a vibrato unlike any other, her vocal waves traveled much further than the stage. When Shakira was a young girl, her father introduced her to an orphanage so that she would be grateful for her own upbringing. After seeing the children that society had turned away, Shakira told herself that she would do something for them when she was older.

Keeping her word, Shakira founded the Pies Descalzos Foundation, which funds schools for underprivileged children throughout Colombia. Also a UN Goodwill Ambassador, Shakira has received numerous awards in honor of dedication to the education of children living below the poverty line.

Cyndi Lauper

Performer of arguably the best song of the '80s—"Girls Just Wanna Have Fun"—singer Cyndi Lauper has had a successful career for over 30 years. Throughout her career, she has has been a loud supporter of the LGBTQ community.

She founded her True Color Fund, which advocates for and promotes equal rights for the LGBTQ community. In 2010, the Fund launched the Give a Damn campaign, which pushes straight people to become more active in fighting for the rights of LGBTQ individuals. Upon discovering that 40 percent of the homeless teen population identified as LGBTQ, Lauper started the Forty to None Project, which provides temporary housing and job search assistance to the LGBTQ homeless youth in New York City.

EVALUATING THE AUTHOR'S ARGUMENTS:

In this viewpoint Kyla Nwede shares the profiles of five women who give time and money in support of a variety of social causes. Have you ever given support to a social cause? How have you done so and what benefit would you say has resulted from your efforts? If you haven't which social issues would you deem worthy of support?

Roosevelt Used His Physical Disability to Advantage

"I think Roosevelt realized this was a strong part of his presence as a candidate, and it was something that actually appealed to people."

National Public Radio

In the following viewpoint National Public Radio (NPR) reports that, contrary to popular belief, the public generally understood that Franklin Delano Roosevelt was suffering from a disability caused by polio. Through the years many people were under the impression that the president hid his disability, largely thanks to Roosevelt's unwillingness to be photographed using mobility aids. The author argues that FDR actually used his condition to further his political career and became a spokesperson for the disease. NPR is an independent, nonprofit media organization that sees its mission as informing the public.

AS YOU READ, CONSIDER THE FOLLOWING QUESTIONS:
1. Did all people contract polio before there was a vaccine for it?
2. Did the public generally know that Franklin D. Roosevelt was disabled by polio, according to the viewpoint?
3. Was FDR's political career affected by his disability, according to NPR?

"Roosevelt's Polio Wasn't a Secret: He Used It to His 'Advantage,'" Fresh Air, November 25, 2013. Fresh Air with Terry Gross is produced in Philadelphia by WHYY Inc. and distributed by NPR. Reprinted by permission.

Americans remember Franklin Delano Roosevelt as the president who led the country through the Great Depression and World War II. He bolstered the nation's spirits with his confidence, strength and optimism, despite being crippled by polio, a disability that's largely invisible in photographs and newsreels of his presidency.

But historian James Tobin says, despite misimpressions to the contrary, Americans of Roosevelt's day were well-aware of his disability. In fact, Tobin says, Roosevelt's struggle to overcome his affliction was an important part of the personal narrative that fueled his political career.

Tobin tells Fresh Air's Dave Davies, "[Roosevelt] only discovered who he really was through the ordeal of polio. ... It gave him a kind of confidence in his own strength that perhaps no one can have until you're tested."

Roosevelt contracted polio at the age of 39, and Tobin's new book explores his battle with the illness and the ways it molded his character and influenced his rise in the Democratic Party. Tobin has written previous books about the Wright brothers and war correspondent Ernie Pyle. His new book is *The Man He Became: How FDR Defied Polio to Win the Presidency*. Interview highlights:

On How Good Sanitation Made Kids More Susceptible to Polio

Before the polio vaccine, pretty much every little kid ingested the polio virus but was protected by maternal antibodies, so even though the virus passed through his or her system, they wouldn't become sick with disease. As sanitation got better, they had fewer immunities, and so if the virus did creep into a community with good sanitation, kids were more likely to get sick and to become seriously ill.

Roosevelt had grown up on an isolated estate in upstate New York. He probably had immune deficiencies to begin with—he was always getting sick with one bug or another. So he was particularly susceptible when, even though he was an adult, he contracted the virus.

President Franklin Delano Roosevelt required mobility aids, such as a wheelchair and crutches, after being stricken with polio. Today, many believe he hid his disability from the public, but in fact he used his celebrity to advocate for similar disabilities.

On FDR's Recovery Efforts

Roosevelt went into a long period of physical rehabilitation after recuperating for several months. By December 1921, he was ready to have a physical therapist begin to massage his muscles, begin to work his muscles, begin to try to figure out exactly the extent of the damage. As more and more time passed in the coming weeks and the early months of 1922, he was able to begin to exercise on his own. This was laborious, difficult: He really could not even stand up on his own at all for months and months, and so this was a matter of lying in his bed, performing these minute little exercises, trying to move one muscle and then another muscle. ... It was painstaking, it was difficult. He had to have his legs put into casts at one point to prevent against contractures. ... It was really a grueling process.

On Misimpressions of FDR's Openness About His Condition

When I've talked to people in the past ... I've always asked them, "Did you know about FDR's condition?" And they've always said yes. What they say is, "We realize later that he was more disabled than we knew, but we certainly knew he was disabled, we knew that he couldn't walk." I think that this misimpression comes from a couple of things:

There was a book published in the 1980s called *FDR's Splendid Deception* in which the writer, Hugh Gregory Gallagher, I think overstated the evidence for FDR covering this up. And then in the debate over the Roosevelt memorial in Washington that took place in the 1990s, that theme got repeated over and over again by various advocates in that argument. And then it got put into a couple of television documentaries, and so it just had a viral effect.

All you have to do is go back to the newspapers of the time, especially from the 1920s when Roosevelt was making his political comeback, and his disability was discussed constantly. He was very frank about it. So there's no question that people knew about it. And you see during his presidency, people who were themselves disabled, people who had polio, their children had polio, writing to FDR in the White House by the hundreds and talking about his disability.

The March of Dimes [nonprofit] itself, which came about during Roosevelt's presidency, he was the leader of it, was an effort to fight polio. The polio campaign that was waged every year had Roosevelt as its figurehead.

On How FDR's Condition Affected His Marriage to Eleanor

I think at first the polio brought the two of them closer together. It was only a few years earlier, 1918, that Eleanor Roosevelt had discovered that he had had this affair with her own social secretary, Lucy Mercer, a situation that everyone knows about. So the marriage had been deeply damaged. Her trust for him had been destroyed.

But polio sort of called upon her to give him all the care that she possibly could give him. That was the sort of wife that Eleanor saw herself as: somebody bound by duty to help her husband. And she absolutely did for many months. She cared for him, she sort of organized his care with physical therapists and nurses at the same time that she was looking after five children and a couple of different households. She really did devote herself to his case.

As he began to pursue his recovery in other places where he could go for treatment, she increasingly saw that she couldn't devote the rest of her life to him and didn't care to. She wanted to express her own individuality, and she wanted to pursue a position of politics of her own, and so she increasingly did that. After 1922 into 1923, they began to lead separate lives, supporting each other in what they were doing but acknowledging they were no longer the kind of husband and wife that they had been before his affair.

On How Roosevelt Worked Around His Condition

Roosevelt realized that when you were crippled—and that was the word that he would use—you have a tendency to make people uncomfortable. People don't know what to say, they don't know where to look, they don't know how to treat you, they don't know whether to feel pity for you, when pity is the last thing that you want. ...

He had to persuade people to feel comfortable in his presence. ... [The therapists and he] began to work on his gait, to work on the way he would walk with the canes and crutches and assistance he would use. So his walk, although slow, began to look more and more natural. And he would seat himself, and he would throw up his head, he would begin to talk—he was always talking, actually—to put people at ease. And this whole physical routine that he developed of putting people at ease was enormously effective, and it made people forget that he was disabled.

On FDR Using His Disability as a Political Advantage

[In a speech in Rochester, N.Y.,] he was talking about the needs of disabled children in the state of New York and he mentions himself. He says, "I myself have been through this ordeal, and I am a symbol of what can happen when people with disabilities are strongly supported."

And nobody had expected him to say this out loud; nobody had expected him to address this issue in this way, to turn the disability on its head and make it into this advantage. And so it had [an] electrifying effect on the audience. ... I think Roosevelt ... realized this was a strong part of his presence as a candidate, and it was something that actually appealed to people.

On Whether His Disability Made Him a Better President

Certainly people close to him said it tempered him. Eleanor herself said it made him stronger and more courageous.

That doesn't quite make sense to me. I think people have those innate capacities or they don't. The crisis draws it out of them. It allows them to see who they really are. And that's why I chose the title *The Man He Became*. I think he was that man before he became sick, but he only discovered who he really was through the ordeal of polio. So it gave him a kind of confidence in his own strength that perhaps no one can have until you're tested.

I also think it inevitably gave him a kind of passion for people who are suffering that he couldn't have had if he had not deeply suffered himself. That capacity was perfectly timed for the country's problems in the Great Depression.

EVALUATING THE AUTHOR'S ARGUMENTS:

In this viewpoint NPR argues that Franklin Delano Roosevelt worked hard to hide the perception of weakness and overcome hardships caused by polio to ultimately advocate for disabilities. How do you think this would have played out today, given the technological advances of social media and the twenty-four-hour news cycle?

Chapter 2

How Have Advancing Media Technologies Impacted the Nature of Fame?

Accessible technology and social media allow anyone to get in the public eye.

Viewpoint

1

"Although it might seem insane, our complete infatuation with celebrities isn't an inexplicable phenomenon."

Social Media Lends Itself to the Development of the Parasocial Relationship

CU Independent

In the following viewpoint authors from CU Independent analyze how celebrity culture affects some people. The authors use the example of a typical fifteen-year-old high-school girl to show how celebrities can make a difference in people's lives. The authors also analyze the concept of "parasocial relationship" and how it plays a role in the phenomenon of celebrity worship. CU Independent, or CUI, is the student news outlet for the University of Colorado at Boulder.

"Opinion: Celebrity Culture Isn't as Harmful as You Think," CU Independent Newspaper, www.cuindependent.com April 26, 2018. Reprinted by permission.

AS YOU READ, CONSIDER THE FOLLOWING QUESTIONS:
  1. According to the viewpoint, is the phenomenon of celebrity
     worship a new thing?
  2. As explained by the authors, what is a "parasocial relationship"
     and how does it affect people?
  3. What age group pays attention to celebrities as stated by the
     authors?

Claire O'Mara is a quiet, polite 15-year-old from Highlands Ranch, Colorado. She's learning how to drive, is an avid kick-boxer and is getting ready to finish her sophomore year of high school.

But if you bash Taylor Swift, she might not be so polite anymore.

O'Mara is a self proclaimed "Swiftie." She first heard Taylor Swift when she was four years old, and that's when she started to fall in love. Through the years, she's developed an affinity for Taylor Swift, including an appreciation for her lyrics and the community that she's found in other fans. Taylor Swift is her role model and idol, and she will always support her, no matter what.

Celebrity worship culture permeates modern society. Celebrities are in advertisements, all over the news and tabloids beg for attention in the grocery store check out lines. Celebrity endorsement doesn't come cheaply, either. In 2012, for example, Beyonce was paid $50 million to promote Pepsi products.

Many Americans complain about celebrity saturation. One study found that 40 percent of Americans believe media gives too much attention to celebrities. However, it doesn't seem as if we can look away.

It's no coincidence that 7.9 million people tuned into watch this season's finale of "The Bachelor," while 2.5 million people, on average, tune into Fox each night during prime-time for news coverage.

Although it might seem insane, our complete infatuation with celebrities isn't an inexplicable phenomenon.

Rick Stevens, a professor in the CMCI department at CU, studies fan culture. According to Stevens, celebrity culture is nothing new.

Is it harmful or beneficial to be a superfan, like Taylor Swift's "Swifties"?

"It relates to earlier conditions or behaviors in which people intensely identified with images and concepts that seemed to transcend their common existence," Stevens said.

We've been admiring those with higher rank in society for thousands and thousands of years. Even in the times of hunter-gatherers, those with the most "material goods" were at the top of the social ladder. In the case of animals, groups look up to the one with the most power.

However, we no longer have to fight for food, and as a result, our biological skills have evolved. According to Psychology Today, because we now have survival figured out, we must look elsewhere. So, we now look up to people that have other things that we desire— to be rich and famous.

The ability to find information about celebrities has only become easier in the digital world. The emergence of social media has lent itself to the development of the "parasocial relationship," which, according to Stevens, is caused by social media's ability to allow the public to look intimately into the lives of celebrities, which might otherwise seem inaccessible. This creates a type of "proxy" relationship. The media presence stands in place of an actual person, which allows the individual to create an interpersonal relationship.

O'Mara claims Taylor Swift feels like a personal friend, even though she's never met her. When she gets the chance to talk about her, she feels excited, passionate — even protective. These are all components of a "real-life" relationship, even though the two have never met, nor do they have any type of direct communication. O'Mara says Swift has bettered her life in more ways than one and has exerted a positive influence on her life.

The parasocial relationship may exist due to social media, but Stevens says we are a culture "obsessed with image and stories." This obsession fosters human connection, and human connection is something we innately crave. The combination of desire for stories as well as human connection creates a space for the parasocial relationship to thrive in modern society.

Because we live in a world dominated by media, there is an awareness of the performance aspect of social media. Celebrities are not exempt from this performance. It could be argued their entire existence is a performance. Stevens asserts this is part of the draw. "We are obsessed with "watch[ing] celebrities closely, looking for signs of the humans behind the performances."

O'Mara's observations about Taylor Swift echo Stevens' analysis.

"Her support through comments on social media have just let us all see that she's a normal person with her own issues just like anyone else; she's not just a big celebrity in my mind," she said.

O'Mara sees the person behind the performance, which allows her to develop a deeper personal connection to Swift and creates the sense of a real relationship.

And while it may be believed celebrity obsession is for teenagers, the age group most heavily influenced by celebrity campaigns is individuals aged 18-37. These individuals reported they were more likely to support a cause because they heard a celebrity advocate for it.

According to Stevens, the admonishment fans get for caring about celebrities isn't quite fair. He claims that celebrity culture is a good thing. Our relationship with celebrities allows us to navigate our heavily mediated world, as stories help us make sense of the world around us.

The stories celebrities share with society not only allow people to connect with them, but also allow them to forge changes in society. O'Mara recounts the lawsuit Taylor Swift was involved in, in which a 51-year-old country music DJ, David Muller, sexually assaulted Swift during a meet and greet in Denver. The jury ruled in favor of Swift, confirming Muller's assault. Muller was then fired, and instead of accepting the offered settlement, Swift decided to make a statement.

In only requesting one dollar in damages, Swift wanted to point out the difference between right and wrong, and hoped to show others that it was not about the money, but rather appropriate behavior. O'Mara explains how the settlement for one dollar is important to her. For her, it retains Swift's true character and identity. From a societal perspective, the case is one in a growing list of sexual assault against women. Those who identify with Swift now have a connection to sexual assault, and may feel empowered to make a difference.

The draw to celebrities is much less superficial than it may appear. The human brain craves connection and stories, and celebrities provide that in the modern world. So, if like O'Mara, you're known as the "Taylor Swift Girl," or something akin, embrace it. Celebrity culture is anything but a modern phenomenon, and the desire to move beyond our own existence is here to stay.

EVALUATING THE AUTHOR'S ARGUMENTS:

In this viewpoint CU Independent maintains that celebrity culture or its infatuation may not be as harmful as one may think. Do you have a celebrity that you greatly admire? Would you say that you feel like you know this celebrity as you would know a close friend? If so, why do you feel close to someone you probably will never meet? If not, what has prevented you from feeling this way?

The Internet Has Launched an Entire Generation of Fame Seekers

Daryl Nelson

"An extremely large portion of kids would rather be Kim Kardashian or Justin Bieber rather than the lawyers and the accountants that manage their brands."

In the following viewpoint Daryl Nelson analyzes why and how so many people are attracted to the idea of becoming famous. Nelson maintains that this modern-day search for celebrity and stardom is actually scary both for individuals and for society. Additionally, the author documents what happens when a person continues with this unrealistic expectation throughout his or her life. Daryl Nelson is a reporter and contributing writer for *Consumer Affairs* and has written for many other online and print publications.

AS YOU READ, CONSIDER THE FOLLOWING QUESTIONS:
1. About how many people want to be famous, according to the viewpoint?
2. According to the author, what do people want to be famous for?
3. What can typically happen to someone pursuing fame through-out life according to the viewpoint?

The new season of *American Idol* kicked off not long ago and while watching the first episode and seeing thousands and thousands of people gathered to get their shot at being a pop star, I was reminded of just how many people want to be famous and live the life of a celebrity.

And although *American Idol* is responsible for laying down that now cemented short path to fame, the huge singing competition is just one out of hundreds that people hope will turn them into the next Carrie Underwood or Jennifer Hudson.

But just why is our modern-day culture so obsessed with fame?

Certainly wanting to be the next big celebrity isn't anything new, as each generation had its portion of wannabe rock, movie and TV stars, but since the rise of the Internet, along with its ability to give the average person an immediate audience, the kid who spent his time gazing at the ceiling dreaming of stardom from his bed, has leapt off the mattress and headed to the nearest computer to show the world what he can do artistically.

What's also different from past generations are the many examples that young people see on television these days of a person going from an unknown to a global sensation seemingly overnight.

It's a little scary, but it seems that an extremely large portion of kids would rather be Kim Kardashian or Justin Bieber rather than the lawyers and the accountants that manage their brands, and what's even scarier is that many of these kids won't just stop at dreaming of fame, some will ignore their personal responsibilities and put more realistic goals, like being a valedictorian, on the back burner.

While most kids have dreamed of becoming stars, it's only recently that fame has seemed attainable.

Famous for Being Famous

Orville Gilbert Brim, author of *Look at Me! The Fame Motive from Childhood to Death*, says that today's culture is full of people who don't want to be famous for a particular talent, they just want to be famous so they can feel better accepted.

Brim pointed to several surveys that showed there are at least 4 million people in the United States who make becoming famous their chief goal in life, and these statistics were pulled from findings in 2009. And one would have to assume those numbers have swelled over the last four years, with even more signing competitions and reality shows being broadcast.

"These millions of people who are so strongly motivated for fame are obviously different from the rest of the population," said Brim in a published interview with the University of Michigan.

"And what has happened is the fame motive has come out of the basic human need for acceptance and approval and when this need is not fulfilled because of rejection by parents, or adolescent peer groups, or others, a basic insecurity develops and emerges as the fame motive."

Brim also differentiates the various ways people hope to become famous, from wanting to achieve celebrity through a great accomplishment, to wanting to be associated with someone who is already famous, like a prominent family or famous actress.

But what's most prominent in today's culture, especially among younger people wanting to be famous, is becoming a celebrity without displaying a talent or putting in any kind of work. Simply put, these folks just want the benefits of being in front of the camera and have no desire of being away from the camera to perfect a craft.

"More in the news these days is what I call 'calls for attention,'" said Brim.

Fame and Renown

"Celebrity comes from the Latin noun meaning 'fame and renown', but these days, it has a new meaning, which designates someone who has become a public figure through seeking media exposure. These persons, which seem to be increasing in number, have done nothing that deserves to be publically praised as an achievement. They're simply calling attention to themselves," he said.

After studying a group of 1,032 sixteen-year-olds, a team of UK researchers determined that more than half had no desire to go into professions that didn't involve being a celebrity.

Some might say this is normal and will eventually fade away, but seeing that the age of 16 is only two years from adulthood, and the age one potentially goes to college, there's a good chance these kids and others like them will bring their fame pursuits into adulthood.

The research team also pointed out that many young people don't know what it takes to apply a talent in order to achieve a respectable kind of notoriety, so many go the faster route and may do things they will regret later in life, like posting an inappropriate or salacious YouTube video.

In a separate study conducted by the Pew Research Center among 18- to 25-year-olds, researchers found that even getting rich is less important than becoming famous among some young people.

Many media experts say the fact that people can be themselves and don't necessarily have to display a talent, makes it seem much less challenging to be on TV these days, so people are even further motiviated to pursue fame.

A Persistent Obsession

What also may sound troubling to some, is the fact that the fame bug is extremely hard to stomp out, and many people will chase unrealistic pursuits their whole lives and most will live in a perpetual state of disappointment, says Brim.

"The fundamental truth about the fame motive is that it's never satisfied and people have to live with it all their lives. However hard they try to become famous, they'll fail to get what they're after," he says.

"This brings many defeats into their lives and later in life, when this final reality sets in, the realization one's never going to become famous, the person must take steps to protect the self from this feeling of failure."

"Some interesting psychological processes occur, what I call 'cognitive strategies,' such as blaming someone else for one's failure, finding new people to compare yourself to who are even less successful, or to the devaluation of others who may have become famous," Brim says.

What's also interesting, says the author, is that the percentage of people wanting to become famous hasn't really increased that much over the years, and it's just the fact that there are more avenues today for people to become celebrities, so it just seems like today's kids want fame more than the kids of past generations.

Brim also points out some interesting figures about the number of people who will be sorely disappointed in their pursuit of fame.

"Out of the 4 million fame seekers, if you look at the Halls of Fame and biographies around the world, there are perhaps only 30,000 entries and of those, perhaps 10,000 are dead," he says.

"So this leaves about 20,000 slots for 4 million fame seekers, which is going to leave 3,980,000 people with no opening where they can be famous."

But I doubt these figures will keep people from trying to be the next Kim Kardashian.

EVALUATING THE AUTHOR'S ARGUMENTS:

In this viewpoint Daryl Nelson accepts that there has always been a certain segment of the population that seeks to be famous, but Nelson contends that the present generation does it for different reasons and in different ways. Give examples of this from the viewpoint and draw conclusions with examples from popular culture and the entertainment industry today.

Viewpoint

3

Television Created the Celebrity Scientist

Declan Fahy

"His fame damaged Sagan's standing in the scientific world."

In the following viewpoint Declan Fahy analyzes the case for scientists becoming celebrities. Fahy uses Carl Sagan, a well-known US scientist, to prove his point. Fahy demonstrates how Sagan became famous and how he suffered in the scientific world because of this fame. Declan Fahy is a professor in the School of Communications at Dublin City University, DCU, in Dublin, Ireland. He has numerous writing credits including a 2015 book, *The New Celebrity Scientists: Out of the Lab and Into the Limelight.*

AS YOU READ, CONSIDER THE FOLLOWING QUESTIONS:
1. According to the author, which two scientists became popular during the 1970's?
2. As reported in the viewpoint, which TV show catapulted Carl Sagan to fame?
3. What happened to Carl Sagan as a result of his celebrity, according to the author?

"Carl Sagan, and the Rise of the 'Celebrity Scientist,'" by Declan Fahy, Rowman & Littlefield, April 30, 2015. Reprinted by permission.

Beginning in 1970, the amount of science reported in the media exploded. In the United States, the 1970s and 1980s saw the creation of science sections in dozens of newspapers across the country, the launch of multiple glossy popular science magazines, and the inauguration of a new weekly television series—*Nova*—devoted to science. Popular science books reached a significant point in the mid-1970s. Before then, there were rarely more than ten titles in the *New York Times* best seller list each year. But afterward, there were rarely fewer than ten best sellers each year. The situation in Britain was similar. Science flowed through popular culture.

Television allowed scientists to speak to vast numbers of citizens. The BBC series *The Ascent of Man* told a science-based story of human history. Broadcast in Britain and the United States in the early 1970s, it was hosted by mathematician and intellectual Jacob Bronowski, who had written and spoken about science to wide audiences in magazines and television long before the show granted him international prominence. During the same decade, across the Atlantic, a planetary scientist was proving himself an engaging media presence, a scientist who would became his era's best-known public scientist: Carl Sagan.

Sagan symbolized an era when the television age met the space age. He was a planetary scientist at a time when space became a proxy battleground for rival Cold War superpowers. He was telegenic at a point where it was clear that television favored personalities, like him, who were articulate, attractive, eloquent, and enthusiastic. He was already well known at the end of the 1970s as a Pulitzer Prize-winning popular science writer who regularly explained astronomy to the hundreds of thousands of nightly viewers of *The Tonight Show* with Johnny Carson.

But when he unveiled the universe to half a billion viewers in the 1980 television series *Cosmos*, he was propelled to unprecedented global fame. Viewers in sixty nations followed the planetary scientist on his 13-part personal odyssey through eons of cosmological and human history. His spin-off book of the series, *Cosmos*, spent more than 70 weeks on the New York Times best seller list and earned him more than $1 million in royalties. *Time* featured Sagan on its cover and called him a "Showman of Science," "the prince of popularizers,"

Before Bill Nye the Science Guy and Neil deGrasse Tyson, there was Carl Sagan, who managed to use his charisma to make science popular. Sagan's stardom came at a cost to his standing in the scientific community, however.

"the nation's scientific mentor to the masses," and "America's most effective salesman of science."

A producer of *Cosmos*, Adrian Malone, vowed to "make Carl a star." And indeed the show led to a surge in media and public attention paid to Sagan. Journalists reported on his personal life, writing about his trademark turtlenecks and his distinctive orange Porsche 914 with its license plate, PHOBOS, one of the moons of Mars. He had to cope with the women who appeared at studios demanding to see him, convinced he spoke directly to them through their television screens. He sometimes sat facing the wall in restaurants to avoid the stream of autograph hunters and well-wishers.

His celebrity brought lucrative rewards. The $2 million he received for *Contact*, his 1985 novel about the scientific search for extraterrestrial life, was, at the time, the largest advance ever given by a publisher for a work not yet in manuscript form. It also brought him influence, granting him a public platform for his anti-nuclear advocacy, as he warned political leaders about the devastation that would occur in the radiation-soaked darkness of a global nuclear winter. Students who watched *Cosmos* wanted to become scientists. No modern scientist had yet achieved such reach, renown, and reputation.

But his fame damaged Sagan's standing in the scientific world. Harvard denied his bid for tenure, a lifetime appointment that a university awards to accomplished scholars. The nation's most prestigious scientific society, the National Academy of Sciences, rejected him as a member. A number of influential peers dismissed him as a mere popularizer and not a real scientist, someone who spent too much time on *The Tonight Show* and too little time engaged in the painstaking grind of observing the planets.

He came to starkly illustrate a feature of modern scientific fame, a feature that critics later called the "Sagan Effect": the perception among researchers that the level of scientists' public fame was in direct opposition to the quality of their research work. Popular scientists, in effect, were not seen as strong scientists. Before his media career, however, Sagan had established a sound reputation as a researcher, known for his pathbreaking work that explained how Venus became boiling hot and violent windstorms raged across the surface of Mars. He accumulated 500 career publications—an astonishing rate of productivity that averaged one published academic paper each month. The Sagan Effect, for Sagan, was false.

FAST FACT

In 1980 Carl Sagan launched his popular TV series, *Cosmos.* In 2014 Neil deGrasse Tyson hosted a reboot of Sagan's famous show.

Not that Sagan was the only scientist to spot the media's enhanced power. He was one of several scientists in US public life in the 1960s and 1970s who saw the media as a way to influence public and political attitudes to science. These "visible scientists"—including anthropologist Margaret Mead, biologist Paul Ehrlich, and chemist Linus Pauling—broke with conventional ways to shape science policy. They bypassed the traditional ways that experts gave behind-the-scenes advice to policymakers. They went directly to the public instead, using the mass media to put science on the public agenda and therefore shape citizen attitudes and, as a result, affect science policy. They showed that the individual scientist working in a cutting-edge area of science, once they were sufficiently articulate, controversial, and distinctive, could attract and hold the media spotlight.

These visible scientists ruptured the conventional ways researchers earned scientific and public attention. As described by a founding father of the sociology of science, Robert K. Merton, an individual scientist's reputation was traditionally established exclusively within science. A scientist gained recognition only after their published research was validated by their peers. The more and better their research, the more their reputation grew, the greater their status in science. The ultimate accolade was the Nobel Prize, the public symbol of scientific excellence, a public award bestowed on those researchers deemed to have produced the world's best science. But Sagan and other visible scientists had a reputation that was in part created outside science. As well as scientific credentials, what also mattered was how they communicated, how engaging they were, how their science was tied to public issues, and how interesting they were as personalities.

EVALUATING THE AUTHOR'S ARGUMENTS:

In this viewpoint Declan Fahy outlines the coming of age of scientific celebrities. He maintains that this celebrity status for scientists really started in the 1970's. Using a previous viewpoint, compare and contrast how celebrities from the entertainment industry and celebrity scientists can cause change.

**Viewpoint
4**

"Although the star system is still vital in shaping who's covered by magazines, the web has destabilised the relationship between the media and the audience."

The Internet Has Changed the Way the Public Interacts with Celebrities

Aleks Krotoski

In the following viewpoint, Aleks Krotoski argues that the rise of the internet and social media have changed the whole system of celebrity and fame. Where once celebrity was carefully controlled by executives, agents, and the celebrities themselves, it now can be in the hands of celebrities and fans, thanks to technology. This can be both freeing and dangerous. Aleks Krotoski has a PhD in the social psychology of relationships in online communities and has been writing about interactivity since 1999.

"What Effect Has the Internet Had on Celebrity?" by Aleks Krotoski, Guardian News and Media Limited, January 23, 2011. Reprinted by permission.

AS YOU READ, CONSIDER THE FOLLOWING QUESTIONS:
1. How has the internet destabilized the relationship between the media and the audience, according to the viewpoint?
2. Why do smartphones and wifi make the public more dangerous to celebrities?
3. According to the author, what is the concern about the quick fame that can now be achieved by ordinary people?

It is the season for Hollywood to celebrate itself in a sycophantic flourish of statuettes, tiaras and tear-stained platitudes. Following the Golden Globes come this week's Oscar nominations and hopefuls will be eyeing up the ballgowns and DJs that their designer friends aim to get on the front pages of the celebrity-spotting magazines. But it won't just be papers and magazines scrutinising the nominations announcement; across much of the internet, a profusion of celebrity-obsessed blogs, forums and websites will also be predicting and predicating, perpetuating our bizarre cultural obsession with all manner of gossip.

As the editor of *Heat* magazine's website, Samuel Pinney, tells me, gossip has always existed. "It just used to be about her at number 42, instead of the latest *X Factor* drop-out."

Indeed, the web pumps out gallons of weirdness about both *X Factor* drop-outs and her at number 42 at the speed of a Google search, so it's not surprising our hunger for useless gossip has been exploited by an ocean of online services that want to capture our attentions. But beyond this proliferation of gossip sites, the web has transformed our relationship with celebrity. Although the star system is still vital in shaping who's covered by magazines, the web has destabilised the relationship between the media and the audience. "It's moved the power over who decides if someone is a celebrity out of the hands of a select few," Pinney says.

The media apparatus that bolstered the ascent of particular personalities to public recognition was highly structured even 15 years ago, according to sociologist P David Marshall, author of *The Celebrity Culture Reader*. Then, a person's "people" drip-fed carefully constructed nuggets of information to a roster of approved outlets.

Without YouTube, it is likely that Logan Paul would be living in obscurity.

Sure, scandals happened and tongues wagged, but now, thanks to long camera lenses and a free-to-access publication platform that reaches around the world, digital technologies have upset the balance of a highly strung industry.

It's because the web works outside the consent of the business. The audience is in charge, armed with a smartphone and a wi-fi connection. This makes us potentially more dangerous to the celebrity than ever before. Then, the worst George Clooney might have faced was a busload of strangers armed with the star maps they got from a hawker in Sunset Boulevard standing outside his well-guarded Beverly Hills fortress. Now fans can zoom into Clooney's backyard on Google Maps or report his most recent location on justspotted. com. And beyond the personal privacy issues, we've also got more control over their careers: then, the duration of their fame was determined by a story arc fabricated by a studio executive; now, the studios have a second-by-second litmus test of a celebrity's worth.

But not only has the web transformed how we interact with our idols, we the audience have also wrested the power to create celebrities from the traditional star-makers. We can now act outside the system, promoting ourselves using similar techniques as the studios, using

FAST FACT

After rapper Kanye West followed ordinary citizen Stephen Holmes on Twitter, Holmes acquired 1,600 new followers overnight.

carefully placed pieces of media and cultivating followings among specifically targeted communities. We can also thrust unwitting people into the spotlight by posting a video on Twitter or Facebook for our friends to see and pass on. Web fame is a moving target and utterly unpredictable.

David Weinberger, fellow at the Harvard Berkman Centre for Internet & Society, thinks the people who are successful at chasing online fame do it by seeking 15 followers, rather than 15 minutes. At a conference about internet trends in 2008, he said it was about cultivating those personal connections by engaging with communities and by getting mentioned on important blogs for your particular shtick.

Unfortunately, the support network built into the experience of offline celebrity that helps to protect the star from the baying masses isn't in place online and the fleeting fame often associated with successful memes or accidental "cewebrities" can often be problematic. Notoriety is a strange bedfellow, thrusting bizarre responsibilities upon people who may suddenly become well known for being the only person followed on Twitter by Kanye West, as was the case with Coventry student Stephen Holmes in the summer of 2010, or for recording a misjudged video of themselves pretending to be a Jedi knight, as happened to Canadian Ghyslain Raza in 2003. Such accidental celebrity can cause unexpected hardship for the person now doorstepped by the global media or bullied into seclusion.

The web offers carte blanche for attention-seekers, whether they are already famous or want to be. Yet online fame is still only second-best. The Star Wars Kid will never be nominated for best supporting actor. But then again, he might forever have some sort of following online and a small but steady income based on guest appearances at supermarket openings. Looking at the career trajectories of some of this week's awards nominees, it may actually be the same thing after all.

EVALUATING THE AUTHOR'S ARGUMENTS:

Viewpoint author Aleks Krotoski writes that "online fame is still only second-best." Do you agree with her assertion? Given what you've read so far, do you think there will come a day when online fame will be more legitimate? What would have to change for that to happen?

The Media Can Help Prevent Copycat Violence and Mass Shooters Seeking Fame

Zaid Jilani

> *"Experts have suggested that shooters are seeking fame as one possible motivation."*

In the following viewpoint Zaid Jilani analyzes the topic of mass shootings through the lens of fame. Jilani argues that there appears to be a correlation between the coverage of mass shootings and the later occurrence of copycat violence. The author notes that there also appears to be some aspect of contagion when it comes to suicide, and for that reason media should be careful how it depicts suicide. Zaid Jilani is a writer for the *Greater Good Magazine* at the University of California at Berkeley.

AS YOU READ, CONSIDER THE FOLLOWING QUESTIONS:

1. Is there a correlation between copycat violence and mass shootings, according to the author?
2. Is suicide contagious, according to the author?
3. According to the viewpoint, how do potential shooters view violence?

"How the Media Can Help Prevent Mass Shootings," by Zaid Jilani, University of California, Berkeley, January 22, 2019. Reprinted by permission.

In the days and weeks following a mass shooting, television news programs saturate audiences with coverage of the tragedy, often focusing on the shooter.

But there's a problem with this approach: It could be making mass shootings more common. According to a recent working paper, intense media coverage of these events may serve to glorify them in the minds of other potential mass shooters, who then seek the same attention by committing similar atrocities.

Jay Walker, an economics professor at Old Dominion University and a coauthor of the study, says that he and economist Michael Jetter wanted to look into the motivations behind mass shootings. "There's been speculation about motives and there's no clear resolution," he notes.

Indeed, some of the most prominent mass shootings of the past decade have left the country puzzled. For instance, after almost a year of investigation, Las Vegas police could determine no motive for a mass shooting that killed 58 people, the deadliest such event in American history.

Experts have suggested that shooters are seeking fame as one possible motivation. By focusing so much coverage on mass shooting events, these experts warn, the news media may be creating incentives for mass shooters, especially when they focus intensely on the individual profiles of the shooters themselves.

But is that true? Walker and Jetter decided to test this hypothesis by analyzing the relationship between the level of news coverage and the occurrence of mass shootings. They picked the popular prime-time news program *ABC World News Tonight* and tracked daily coverage from January 1, 2013 to June 23, 2016.

Shockingly, they found a positive and statistically significant relationship between the amount of coverage dedicated to mass shootings and the number of shootings that occurred in the following week.

"At its mean," the researchers conclude, "ABC news coverage is suggested to cause approximately three mass shootings in the subsequent week, equivalent to 58 percent of mass shootings in the United States." (Their results were robust using both definitions of a "mass shooting": either four or more individuals shot and four or more individuals killed.)

Is there a degree of contagion caused by media coverage and depiction of mass shootings and suicides?

"We find a pretty clear empirical relationship between coverage and future acts," says Walker. But their work also hints at solutions. More than just reducing coverage, say experts, we all need to change the way we think about mass shootings.

How Much Is Too Much?

Although the relationship between TV news coverage and mass shootings has been studied before, the Walker-Jetter study introduced a novel innovation. To isolate causality between television news coverage and mass shootings, they also compared it to the occurrence of natural disasters. They found that news media coverage of shootings decreased during natural disasters, which was associated with fewer shootings the following week.

"You've got these natural disasters that crowd out coverage of the shootings when they occur," Walker says. "And then in the future there are future shootings that happen in the near term."

Walker and Jetter did not study the composition of news coverage of mass shootings, only the amount. Thus they could not offer any recommendations for how to change coverage, but Walker argues that it's important to not oversaturate individual shootings with coverage.

There's another good reason to reduce coverage of mass shootings: They are rare. There were four times as many students shot and killed in schools in the early '90s compared to today; on average, around ten students a year are killed in school shootings, out of the 56 million students who attend public and private primary and secondary education schools. More children every year are killed in bicycle accidents and pool drownings than in school shootings.

This does not mean that it's not worth the news media covering the topic of gun violence and probing possible solutions. But media can do that by discussing the wider issue rather than focusing on individual tragedies in a way that may unnecessarily increase public anxiety—and glamorize the shooters.

Lessons from Suicide Prevention

Jetter and Walker suggest that media can learn a lot from research into suicide contagion, the idea that exposure to a suicide can lead to an increase in suicidal behavior.

For instance, when the Netflix series *13 Reasons Why* debuted—which depicted the aftermath of a teen's suicide—mental health researchers critically examined the film, worried that it might create suicide contagion by glorifying the act of self-harm. One study did in fact find an association between watching the show and suicidal thoughts; another showed a spike in Google searches for suicide following the show's release; yet another discovered that having seen the show led at-risk youth to think more about killing themselves.

Dr. Dan Reidenberg, a psychologist and the executive director of Suicide Awareness Voices of Education (SAVE), was one of the critics of 13 Reasons and is an advocate for changing the way the news media report on acts of violence like suicide and mass shootings.

"We want to make sure that the alleged perpetrator is not overly talked about," he says.

Nicole Smith Dahmen, a journalism professor at the University of Oregon who studies visual representation in media, agrees. "We know from research that the way mass shootings are covered can have a contagion effect the same way that suicides can have a contagion effect, so that's very dangerous," she says. "When it comes to covering mass shootings and gun violence, we want to emphasize the victims, we want to tell the stories of the community, and recovery, and resilience, rather than focusing on the perpetrator."

Dahmen and Reidenberg's conclusion is that intensely profiling mass shooters themselves could inspire more of them, because potential shooters will see violence as a way to quickly gain fame.

In 2017, SAVE put out comprehensive guidelines for reporting on mass shootings. These guidelines offer specific advice for minimizing "copycat" behavior by other potential shooters.

SAVE suggests, for instance, that media use the perpetrator's photo "sparingly." When they do publish the photo, news media should crop out imagery of weapons or uniforms, which are visual elements that may inspire copycats. Media should not sensationalize individual acts of violence in a way that may "encourage people who may seek notoriety." SAVE advises television news anchors to not call a shooting the "deadliest incident since Columbine," for example. In other words, media should not cover shootings like football, as a kind of competition.

Dahmen suggests that the news media can focus on solutions and on how communities are recovering rather than focusing solely on individual acts of violence.

"This is a chance for things like solutions reporting," Dahmen said. "What are some potential solutions to gun violence, to mass shootings? Look at what communities are doing to recover and move on."

Chapter 3

Is the Influence of Celebrity Culture on Society Dangerous?

Recording moments for social media has replaced simply enjoying life experiences.

Viewpoint

1

"How can we possibly explain the seemingly useless interest that we have in the lives of reality-show contestants, movie stars, and public figures?"

Caring About Others Was Once Necessary for Survival

Frank T. McAndrew

In the following viewpoint Frank T. McAndrew maintains that humans are biologically primed to pay attention to those around them and especially to gossip about others. McAndrew provides numerous examples why this behavior was socially acceptable, and he argues that it was necessary for the survival of early humans. Frank T. McAndrew is a professor of psychology at Knox College in Galesburg, Illinois. His articles have appeared in many places including the *New Yorker, CNN, Scientific American*, and many others.

AS YOU READ, CONSIDER THE FOLLOWING QUESTIONS:
1. According to the author, what makes the Kardashians celebrities?
2. How are humans made to be gossipers, as explained in the viewpoint?
3. What good comes to teens from celebrity watching, according to the author?

"Why Caring About Celebrities Can Be Good for You," by Frank T. McAndrew, Psychology Today, Sussex Publishers, LLC, March 16, 2015. Reprinted by permission.

More people than ever before are puzzling over the 24/7 coverage of people such as the Kardashian sisters, who are "celebrities" for no other apparent reason than we happen to know who they are.

And yet we can't look away.

Coverage of these individuals' lives continues because people are obviously tuning in.

Although many social critics have bemoaned this explosion of popular culture as reflecting some kind of collective character flaw, it is in fact nothing more than the inevitable outcome of the collision between 21st-century media and Stone Age minds. When you cut away its many layers, our fixation on popular culture reflects an intense interest in the doings of other people; this preoccupation with the lives of others is a byproduct of the psychology that evolved in prehistoric times to make our ancestors socially successful.

Thus, it appears that we are hardwired to be fascinated by gossip.

How could an obsession with celebrities have anything to do with our evolution as human beings?, you may ask.

Well, if we think in terms of what it would have taken to be successful in our prehistoric social environment, the idea may not seem quite so far-fetched. As far as scientists can tell, our prehistoric ancestors lived in relatively small groups in which they knew everyone else in a face-to-face, long-term kind of way. Strangers were probably an infrequent and temporary phenomenon.

Our ancestors had to cooperate with so-called in-group members for success against out-groups, but they also had to recognize that these same in-group members were their main competitors when it came to dividing limited resources. Living under such conditions, our ancestors faced a number of consistent adaptive problems, such as remembering who was a reliable, trustworthy person and who was a cheater; knowing who would be a reproductively valuable mate; and figuring out how to successfully manage friendships, alliances, and family relationships.

The social intelligence needed for success in this environment required an ability to predict and influence the behavior of others; an intense interest in the private dealings of other people would have been handy indeed, and strongly favored by natural selection. In

There may be a psychological reason why we are so interested in celebrities, reality TV stars, and others we don't really know.

short, people fascinated with the lives of others were simply more successful than those who were not, and it is the genes of those busy-bodies that have come down to us through the ages.

OK, so we can explain the intense interest that we have in other people who are socially important to us. But how can we possibly explain the seemingly useless interest that we have in the lives of real-ity-show contestants, movie stars, and public figures of all kinds?

One possible explanation may be found in the fact that celebrity is a relatively recent phenomenon, evolutionarily speaking. In our ancestral world, any person about whom we knew intimate details of his or her private life was, by definition, socially important to us.

Anthropologist Jerome Barkow of Dalhousie University in Canada has pointed out that evolution did not prepare us to distin-guish among members of our community who have genuine effects on our life and the images and voices we are bombarded with by the entertainment industry. Thus, the intense familiarity with celebrities provided by the modern media trips the same gossip mechanisms that have evolved to keep up with the affairs of in-group members. After all, anyone whom we see that often and know that much about must be socially important to us. News anchors and television actors we see every day in soap operas become as familiar as neighbors.

In the modern world, celebrities may serve another important social function.

In a highly mobile, industrial society, they may be the only "friends" we have in common with new neighbors and coworkers. Think of them as "friends-in-law." They provide a common interest and topic of conversation between people who otherwise might not have much to say to one another, and they facilitate the types of informal interactions that help people become comfortable in new surroundings.

Hence, keeping up with the lives of actors, politicians, and athletes can make a person more socially adept during interactions with strangers and even provide segues into social relationships with new friends in the virtual world of the Internet.

Research published in 2007 by Belgian psychologist Charlotte De Backer from the University of Antwerp (full disclosure: I was a coauthor) finds that young people even look to celebrities and popular culture for learning life strategies that would have been learned from role models within one's tribe long ago. Teenagers in particular seem to be prone to learning how to dress, how to manage relationships, and how to be socially successful in general by tuning in to popular culture.

Thus, gossip is a more complicated and socially important phenomenon than we think. When it is discussed seriously, the goal usually is to suppress the frequency with which it occurs in an attempt to avoid the undeniably harmful effects it can have in work groups and other social networks. This tendency, however, overlooks that gossip is part of who we are and an essential part of what makes groups function as well as they do.

Perhaps it may be more productive to think of gossip as a social skill rather than as a character flaw, because it is only when we do not do it well that we get into trouble.

In short, I believe we will continue to shake our heads at what we are constantly subjected to by the mass media, rationally dismissing it as irrelevant to anything that matters in our own lives. But in case you find yourself becoming just a tiny bit intrigued by some inane story about a celebrity, let yourself off the hook: After all, it is only human nature.

EVALUATING THE AUTHOR'S ARGUMENTS:

Viewpoint author Frank T. McAndrew maintains that paying attention to celebrities and taking part in gossip may be positive to people both in modern times and from history. Does this seem counterintuitive to you? Does the author's argument change your opinion? Why or why not?

Viewpoint 2

Celebrity Culture Can Be Used Productively in the Development of Young People

Kirsty Fairclough

"Many young people are more than capable of making informed, intelligent choices about which celebrities they follow."

In the following viewpoint Kirsty Fairclough maintains that some experts and parents contend there is a definite link between unhealthy behaviors in young people as a direct result of the celebrity role models they follow, while in other cases, young people are not affected or actually may show some form of positive benefit. Fairclough points out that this issue of poor role model equals poor behavior outcome of followers is misleading and too generalized and instead it is a complex issue which needs more clarity. Kirsty Fairclough is a senior lecturer in media and performance at the University of Salford in Manchester, England.

AS YOU READ, CONSIDER THE FOLLOWING QUESTIONS:
1. According to the author, which celebrity is a preferred role model for young girls?
2. What is a health issue linked to celebrity culture as explained by the viewpoint?
3. According to the viewpoint, do all young people idolize celebrities?

The recent 2015 MTV Video Music Awards event was notable—not for the recognition of award recipients, but for the public spat between host Miley Cyrus and hip-hop artist Nicki Minaj. Whether real or staged, the hurling of insults and aggressive behaviour dominated mainstream press coverage of the ceremony surely much to the delight of MTV.

Both Minaj and Cyrus are known for courting controversy and have been criticised for being "bad" role models for young people, particularly girls and young women. But what if the mainstream media considered that young people actually use incidents such as this and celebrity culture in a wider sense in a whole host of complex ways to negotiate their identities?

A well-publicised survey of UK parents with children under ten years old voted both Cyrus and Minaj as the worst role models for their daughters. This came even before the recent spat.

The dislike of Minaj and Cyrus appears to be centred on their penchant for dressing provocatively and being outspoken about their sexuality. In predictable contrast, the Duchess of Cambridge was considered the most positive influence on young girls. The worst male offenders were musicians and performers Kanye West, Justin Bieber and former One Direction band member Zayn Malik.

Obsessed with Celebrity

Discourse in this vein is not a new phenomenon. Musicians and performers have long been considered to influence young people in negative ways. In the 21st century, the impact of celebrity culture on society, especially on young people, has come under scrutiny.

The idolization of celebrities is nothing new. But can celebrity culture be used as a teaching tool for young people?

Are today's youth obsessed with celebrity? Is this detrimental to society? Can celebrities ever have a positive influence on young people? Does celebrity culture really matter? These are complex and plural questions to which there are few, if any, concrete answers. However, what is routinely ignored in mainstream media is young people's sense of agency.

Much of the research and commentary surrounding such questions is centred on how celebrity culture may impact upon health and well being in terms of eating disorders or mental health issues.

The rise and dominance of social media sites such as Instagram and their links to the glorification of "super-skinny" celebrities have been cited as influences in the rise of eating disorders in young people.

The British Psychological Society recently said experts warned that youngsters are finding it increasingly difficult to cope with images permeating from a celebrity culture in which thin bodies are celebrated, larger ones are ridiculed and children are sexualised.

Sense of Identity

It is logical to suggest that continual exposure to celebrity culture impacts in negative ways on some young people's senses of identity. This may well affect health and well being, but how this happens and to what degree is incredibly complex. We must also consider the ways in which the media choose to present rather narrow ideas about how celebrities—particularly female ones—should behave and how they should look.

Those whose behaviour falls outside of these narrow ideas are often condemned as being wayward, controversial and difficult. Indeed young people may well negotiate their own gendered identities through the celebrity and by talking about them with their peers. The Celeb Youth project in the United Kingdom is an excellent example of much needed academic research into the field of celebrity and identity. It focused on the influence of celebrities in the construction of young people's aspirations.

What is omitted from the media conversation about celebrities as role models is that many young people are more than capable of making informed, intelligent choices about which celebrities they follow and are becoming increasingly aware of the ways in which the media positions celebrities against each other in terms of race and class.

Young people may connect with those that they feel best represent them as well as those that do not. Indeed, it is also fair to suggest that many young people have no interest in celebrity culture at all.

It is the active and complex use of celebrity culture by young people to negotiate the world around them that is often lost in favour of sweeping generalisations about negative impacts. Perhaps rather than eliminating celebrity culture from the classroom, it could be used productively and constructively to allow young people to make sense of the world they are growing up in.

EVALUATING THE AUTHOR'S ARGUMENTS:

In this viewpoint Kirsty Fairclough reports that the issue of whether celebrity culture negatively impacts young people is not a simple one. But there appears to be a link between media coverage and exultation of skinny celebrities and with it a tendency for young women to have eating disorders. Have you ever wished your body size was more like that of a model or TV star? How does this thinking impact your life?

Viewpoint

3

"As social media has proved that people can be successful with no obvious qualifications or training scientific expertise might arguably be eroded."

Celebrity Non-Experts Could Change the Way We Acquire Knowledge

Ashley Morgan

In the following viewpoint Ashley Morgan reports on an obvious negative aspect of the proliferation of social media. Morgan provides examples of celebrities that have remade themselves as "experts" when they lack any training or credentials to claim expert status. Morgan points out a terrible problem—how can facts and true experts be found among the legions of fake posers. Ashley Morgan is a senior lecturer at the Cardiff School of Art and Design at Cardiff Metropolitan University in the United Kingdom.

AS YOU READ, CONSIDER THE FOLLOWING QUESTIONS:
1. What are celebrities remaking themselves as, according to the viewpoint?
2. Which celebrity promotes her pseudoscience health and beauty corporation as explained by Morgan?
3. According to the author, is pseudoscience based on opinion or fact?

When digital media entrepreneur Andrew Keen predicted in 2007 that the user generated focus of Web 2.0 would lead to a reduction of well researched and factual information—and in turn the rise of amateur opinion—he was clearly on to something.

Over a decade later, and Keen's prognosis has, arguably, come true. The internet today is a source of seemingly endless amounts of easily digestible material. Countless people contribute to its "factual" information, and promote their own opinions as facts too. Through Facebook, Twitter and Instagram, people—particularly celebrities—are also able to promote products and ideas in a much more immediate and visual way. And to frame or reinvent themselves as experts in completely different areas than the ones they gained fame in.

Amateur Experts

While people have long modelled and promoted fashionable clothing, for example, a number of celebrities have taken this idea further in the past ten years. They have broken away from the activities that made them famous—acting, singing, or sport—and reinvented themselves as business people. They are now more than just promoters of certain products, nor those whose style should merely be copied. They are the "go to" for fashionable lifestyles.

That celebrities are moving into business is not such a surprise. Yet, the way in which they adopt expertise in matters on which they have no training is a new twist in the rise of the amateur. Spice Girl Victoria Beckham, is now a fashion designer, for example, and actress Gwyneth Paltrow is a lifestyle and "health" guru. When Beckham

Many worried about the impact of celebrity culture when reality TV star Donald Trump was elected president in 2016.

first launched her clothing line in 2008, fashion editors were ready to be sceptical, but influential magazines such as Harper's Bazaar and Vogue were impressed. Despite no apparent training in design—her initial "expertise" in this matter came from her personal interest in clothing and being photographed wearing fashionable clothes—Beckham recently celebrated a decade as a fashion designer.

Similarly, Paltrow's "modern lifestyle brand" GOOP sells face creams and other products under the umbrella of health and beauty. These are endorsed by Paltrow herself, and contributing doctors help advocate the so-called medicinal aspects of some of her products. Despite the chorus of criticism against Paltrow and GOOP's "psuedo-science," the company is now reportedly worth US$250m.

Fame and Facts

Using the internet as a tool to promote celebrity has also worked for erstwhile businessman Donald Trump. Despite never having held a position as state governor (the common route to political power and presidency), and having no political expertise, Trump was able to become US president. Not least his ascendance was due to a social media campaign that relied on reproducing his "plain talking" rather than political rhetoric.

These new experts don't even have to be famous for another reason to demonstrate expertise. Ella Mills, for example, is a UK blogger who, through documenting her illness and experimenting with food, became a staunch advocate of "clean eating" (although she has since tried to distance herself from the term). This helped launch her "natural and honest" food brand, Deliciously Ella, without any experience as a dietitian.

Now anyone with a Twitter or Instagram account and an opinion can promote expertise, and celebrities can interact directly with fans, showing them how to emulate their own impressive lives.

While social media can be considered a force for good in education, the dominance of a point of view approach in this sphere—rather than true expertise—could have a negative impact on expert knowledge itself, and the idea that you spend time to train and gain qualifications in a chosen field before claiming expertise.

As more people turn to the internet and social media for information of all kinds, it might arguably be much harder to tell point of view from empirical and factual research, as they now both appear in the same place. A recent example of this is the wider proliferation of pseudoscience. Pseudoscience itself is based on amateur opinions, and the issue with this is that social media becomes the supreme platform for perpetuating it. It is very easy to find information that confirms a point of view rather than challenges it.

As social media has proved that people can be successful with no obvious qualifications or training, and point of view increasingly confirms people's perspectives, scientific expertise might arguably be eroded. And as social media produces financial incentives through marketing opportunities, the power of these "experts" could gain strength, creating a whole new shift in the acquisition of knowledge. Keen originally predicted that rather than widening and diversifying knowledge, interactive media would inevitably lead to digital narcissism and an increasing narrowing of the self. While many people have benefited financially and in terms of social status, the quality of knowledge that has emerged from social media is increasingly narrow and difficult to gauge.

EVALUATING THE AUTHOR'S ARGUMENTS:

In this viewpoint Ashley Morgan analyzes a negative aspect of social media, that opinions and pseudoscience can pose as fact and expert knowledge when disseminated by people who have the public's ear for other reasons. What is the danger in this trend? How can this affect people?

Viewpoint 4

Parents, Not Celebrities, Need to Remain Role Models for Their Children

"It is important that children do not develop an obsessive attachment to celebrities by using them as their only role models."

Anne Steinhoff

In the following viewpoint Anne Steinhoff analyzes the media driven world of celebrities and how they often become role models to children at a young age. The author argues that there are both positive and negative issues for this behavior and provides demonstrable examples. Anne Steinhoff is a PhD candidate at the University of Essex, United Kingdom, and blogs for the Novak Djokovic Foundation.

AS YOU READ, CONSIDER THE FOLLOWING QUESTIONS:
1. According to the author, what is one negative consequence of children having celebrities as role models?
2. What is a positive aspect of children having celebrities as role models?
3. According to the viewpoint, how should parents talk to their children about celebrity behavior?

"The Influence of Celebrities on Children's Upbringing," by Anne Steinhoff, Novak Djokovic Foundation, August 2, 2016. Reprinted by permission.

C hildren's ability to imitate the actions of others is a very powerful form of learning because it prompts parental interaction and helps children to learn about the social environment. In today's media-focused world, however, children rather look up to or even become obsessed with celebrities rather than their parents. Although, there is nothing wrong with idolizing singers, movie stars or sports figures, it is important that children do not develop an obsessive attachment to celebrities by using them as their only role models.

A Celebrity-Driven Media World

TV series and social media have created a celebrity-driven environment in which children start to fixate on famous athletes or music stars from an early age. Children are attracted to series and commercials that present a life that seems to be much more colourful and interesting than their own. Unsurprisingly, youngsters mimic and absorb the images on the screen interpreting them as reality. For instance, if a child's favourite singer advertises an accessory or clothes, children will value their opinion much more than that of a parent or relative and see the product as a necessity in order to bound with their idol. It may become difficult to change their mind about the particular product and trying persistently may even just lead to the child to dig deeper into wanting the item.

Negative Influences

Changing children's opinions about celebrities becomes even more difficult when children already have an obsessive fixation on their idol and see them as their primary role model. This is a particular problem when celebrities are engaging in poor behaviour in public. Some actors who play roles in teen TV shows may dress inappropriately in their free time or on the red carpet contributing to a wrong body image or outward appearance for youngsters. Picking up an unhealthy diet from a celebrity who is seen in public eating fast food all the time is another example of bad celebrity influence and there are many more disrespectful and even dangerous behaviours children can pick up from them.

Parents can steer their children's interest from singers and actors to inspirational figures who have more substance, such as youth environmental activist Greta Thunberg.

Positive Influences

However, not all celebrities have a negative impact on the world of their youngest fans. There are many celebrities who use their publicity to support charities, increase awareness of diseases or make donations. There are also many sport figures who give an inside into their difficult journeys and share their personal sacrifices to achieve success in sport. These stars can be very good role models to children and are an inspiration. They can have a positive influence on children in order to do well in school, give back to the community by volunteering or donating toys and may be an inspiration to achieve more in life than participating in a reality show or earn a fortune. As with all celebrities and particularly with the youngest ones, it's worth keeping an eye on their activities to be up to date on their public engagements and to hear about any changes in their social behaviour as soon as possible.

Finding Good Role Models

It is important to understand what kind of impact celebrities have on children's life in order to help them not to copy poor behaviour just because someone famous they like engages in such behavior. Children may not understand that their favourite actor is only playing a role in a TV series and has an entirely different personality when he or she is off-camera. Therefore, parents need to help children to realise that their idol only portrays a character in a series and engage in a conversation with them to help them determining what makes a good role model. There is nothing wrong enjoying a

singer's music or an actor's series even if they are involved in bad behaviour outside their career but it is crucial to discuss the consequences of their bad choices that lead to fines or bad publicity. When talking to children about their favourite celebrities, conversations can be steered into the direction to understand why they like a particular celebrity much more than another. This way, parents can gain an insight into the values of their children. These conversations are also an opportunity to introduce children to much cooler role models who have attributes that are admirable. It could be a celebrity who donates to a charity or raises poverty awareness. Older children may also be interested in famous role models who have accomplished a lot at their young age such as Malala Yousafzai who is a global leader for female education and received the Nobel Peace Prize. Regardless to whom a child looks up to, it is important to make sure that they understand to value their own uniqueness and talents, and pursue a life they like rather than following someone else's.

EVALUATING THE AUTHOR'S ARGUMENTS:

In this viewpoint Anne Steinhoff analyzes the issue of celebrity role models and how it affects the behavior of young people. Do you see yourself as having a celebrity role model? What kinds of influences have affected you because of this? Do you feel it is negative or positive?

Viewpoint

5

"Young people believe celebrities have an effect on the way people think more than politicians, scientists or academics."

Endorsements by Celebrities Have an Impact on Politics

Nives Zubcevic-Basic

In the following viewpoint Nives Zubcevic-Basic dissects the issue of celebrity endorsements. The author analyzes the different kinds of endorsements that occur, and how they affect various population groups. Celebrity endorsements are particularly influential when it comes to politics and voting, and they have been for a long time. Nives Zubcevic-Basic is a lecturer at Swinburne University of Technology in Melbourne, Australia.

AS YOU READ, CONSIDER THE FOLLOWING QUESTIONS:

1. According to the viewpoint, are celebrity political endorsements a new thing?
2. How else do celebrities make endorsements as reported by the author?
3. What traits make good celebrity quality according to the author?

Celebrities are always part of the show in the US presidential election. This is by no means a new trend. Historians have traced the role of celebrities in politics back to the 1920 election, when Warren Harding was endorsed by film stars including Lillian Russell.

In 1960, John F. Kennedy was endorsed by Rat Pack members Sammy Davis junior and Dean Martin. More recently, Oprah Winfrey, George Clooney, will.i.am, Brad Pitt and Samuel L. Jackson supported Barack Obama. Actor Clint Eastwood, however, endorsed Republicans John McCain in 2008 and Donald Trump this time around.

The 2016 election is no different. So how much of a difference, if any, do high-profile endorsements make? And to which demographics?

Who's Endorsing Who?

Both Hillary Clinton and Donald Trump have been endorsed by an army of celebrity supporters.

Some of Clinton's high-profile endorsers include LeBron James, Amy Schumer, Katy Perry, Meryl Streep, Jamie Lee Curtis, Lady Gaga, Ellen DeGeneres, Drew Barrymore, George Clooney, Khloe Kardashian, Kerry Washington, Viola Davis, Britney Spears, John Legend, Richard Gere, Salma Hayek, Lena Dunham, Jennifer Lopez, Beyonce and Snoop Dogg.

In contrast, some of Trump's supporters include Azealia Banks, Sarah Palin, Kirstie Alley, Tom Brady, Charlie Sheen, Dennis Rodman, Kid Rock, Mike Tyson, Donnie Wahlberg, Gary Busey, Hulk Hogan, Tim Allen and Chuck Norris.

If we simply look at the Twitter power behind some of the celebrities listed above, Clinton's camp—with DeGeneres, Spears, James, Lopez and Beyonce—has a combined 195.6 million followers, compared to Trump's camp—Sheen, Tyson, Palin, Hogan and Alley—with a combined 21 million followers.

Celebrities often go beyond simple endorsements and make powerful statements such as Elizabeth Banks' Fight Song or the star-studded Avengers cast's oblique but powerful statement against Trump.

A political endorsement from someone as influential as Oprah Winfrey can carry a lot of weight.

Celebrities Sell

Advertisements featuring celebrities are a popular marketing strategy. In fact, one in five ads globally features a celebrity. Undoubtedly, endorsements are big business.

Some well-known campaigns include Beyonce and Pepsi (worth US$50 million), Justin Bieber and OPI nail polish ($12.5 million) and Brad Pitt and Chanel No. 5 ($6.7 million).

Marketers happily spend millions on celebrity endorsers as they are able to leverage "secondary brand associations"—that is, people transfer their opinions and feelings about a celebrity to the brand.

In a cluttered world where myriad messages fight for the attention of time-starved consumers, celebrity endorsers serve as arbiters of public opinion. And so, marketing organisations rely on symbolic and emotional features to generate "sociopsychological associations". Some celebrities are seen to be so aspirational that even a glimpse of them in an ad conveys positive meaning, like athletes Cristiano Ronaldo and Roger Federer.

It's important to understand the traits a celebrity, also referred to as a source, should have in order to transfer positive meaning to a

brand. These are broken down into three categories:

• source attractiveness (physique, intellect, athleticism, lifestyle);
• source credibility (expertise, trustworthiness); and
• meaning transfer (compatibility between brand and celebrity).

Quite often, celebrities use their high profile to encourage people, world organisations and politicians to support their cause, like singer Bono's One campaign against poverty. Actors Jack Black and Neil Patrick Harris encouraged Californians to vote against the California Marriage Protection Act.

Not-for-profit and world organisations are aware of the power of celebrities and create connections in order to garner publicity, awareness and donations. This includes the United Nations and Angelina Jolie, and DeGeneres and the Ice Bucket Challenge.

Celebrity Endorsements in Politics Makes Sense

We know celebrities grab and hold consumer attention. They also improve ad recall. People are more likely to think positively about a product because they are familiar with the celebrity.

However, expertise is an important element when wanting to influence consumers. Credibility is another crucial factor that tells us not all celebrities are equal. Those considered to be more credible have a higher influence on people's opinions and decisions.

Celebrities with prior political activism, like Martin Sheen and George Clooney, are more likely to have a stronger influence. Interestingly, people consider celebrities to be more credible and trustworthy than politicians.

A negative comment by a credible endorser such as Oprah Winfrey can be as damaging as a positive one. For example, Winfrey stopped eating burgers during the 1996 "mad cow" spread—this resulted in a 10% drop in cattle futures the next day.

Effectiveness and Audience

Research has found that young adults are more likely to listen to family and friends, rather than celebrities, as a source of political information.

At the same time, young people believe celebrities have an effect on the way people think—more than politicians, scientists or academics. Outside of age, ethnicity and gender are also known to affect celebrity endorsement influence.

For instance, African-American and Caucasian-American voters are more likely to rely on family and friends. However, Asian-American, Polynesian and Hispanic voters are more likely to trust politicians or interest groups. Also, men consider celebrities to have a greater influence than women do, regardless of cultural background.

Celebrities are able to motivate young people to seek further information and to take part. However, this is less true of first-time voters. Those who are less politically savvy or poorly informed are also more likely to vote for a political party endorsed by a celebrity.

What's interesting is that most celebrities tend to align themselves with politically uncontroversial issues and tend to steer towards liberal perspectives—for example, George Clooney and Not On Our Watch, a campaign for improving human rights.

Trump's camp includes controversial celebrities who have previously been involved in controversial branding endorsements, like Charlie Sheen and underwear brand Hanes.

Trump was also a celebrity prior to becoming a candidate. People's experience of his public persona through his roles on TV have over time instilled a specific meaning. That meaning is now transferred to his political campaign.

So What's the Final Verdict?

With the right celebrity endorsements, political campaigns can do quite well.

Oprah Winfrey's endorsement of Obama in 2008 was found to increase overall voter participation and number of contributions received by Obama, and an estimated overall 1 million additional votes.

All it takes is trustworthiness, credibility, and a lot of followers.

EVALUATING THE AUTHOR'S ARGUMENTS:

In this viewpoint Nives Zubcevic-Basic paints a picture of celebrity endorsements and how they affect a multitude of issues in the United States, including politics. What types of products have you purchased because they were endorsed by a celebrity? Did the product live up to its endorsement? Would a celebrity's political endorsement influence you? Why or why not?

Viewpoint

6

Our Fascination with Fame Is in Overdrive

"We need to ask ourselves what value we assign to the people who dominate what is starting to feel like every aspect of our lives."

Anna Pivovarchuk

In the following viewpoint Anna Pivovarchuk argues that the public's obsession with celebrity, while nothing new, has escalated in recent years thanks to the almost overwhelming quantity of content. Celebrity magazines, entertainment news shows and websites, reality shows, social media—there are many more ways for the public to get their fix. This can have a negative impact, asserts the author, particularly on young people who may use celebrity worship as an escape and fame as a personal goal. Anna Pivovarchuk is the cofounder and deputy managing editor of Fair Observer.

AS YOU READ, CONSIDER THE FOLLOWING QUESTIONS:

1. Who is credited with saying "In the future, everyone will be world-famous for fifteen minutes"?
2. What did preteens say was the number one goal for their future, according to a study conducted by UCLA?
3. What popular band declared they were more popular than Jesus?

When you think of the nature of celebrity, almost infallibly the first thing that comes to mind is the concept of "15 minutes of fame." Coined at the end of the transformative 1960s, "In the future, everyone will be world-famous for 15 minutes" became Andy Warhol's best-known statement. It is completely insignificant that he allegedly admitted to never having used the phrase.

With the overwhelming upsurge in various types of mass media today, Warhol's quip seems to ring truer than ever. Endless reality-TV shows, celebrity gossip magazines and websites with an annual revenue of more than $3 billion, and a global movie industry have created a conveyor belt of people who, in the words of cultural historian Daniel Boorstin, are "well-known for their well-knowness." As these celebrities multiply and become more available to their audience, the cultural paradigm appears to shift toward the superficial and the sensationalist—a generational lament of loss of enduring value.

We have a desire to idolize. We compulsively follow the everyday lives of celebrities, from the tragic, like their heartbreaks and deaths, to the mundane, like what kind of coffee they drank that morning. The personal aspects of people's lives matter more than their professional achievements. Preoccupation with the image is reaching unprecedented proportions: More than 40 billion photos have been shared on Instagram since it launched in 2010, with around 95 million uploaded daily by its 700 million users. Our fascination with the visual is the Mona Lisa for the digital age.

So, what effects does celebrity admiration, or worship, have on society?

Psychologists in the early 2000s described the syndrome (CWS) as having various degrees of severity. These range from entertainment-social, the usual interest in celeb gossip we share with friends; to intense-personal, where some may experience feelings of bereavement similar to losing a loved one in case of a favorite celebrity's death; to borderline-pathological, which include conditions such as erotomania, where an individual has delusions that someone of a higher social status, very often a celebrity, is in love with them.

Studies have shown a correlation between adolescents who worship celebrities do not just mimic their style, but opt for plastic surgery

Kim Kardashian earned hundreds of millions of dollars from an app that allowed fans a peek inside her life.

more often than those who do not worship celebs. The American Society of Aesthetic Plastic Surgery estimates that between 33,000 to 65,000 children below 18 undergo cosmetic surgery each year, with nonsurgical cosmetic procedures ranging from 91,000 to 190,000 annually.

A study by UCLA's Children's Digital Media Center @ LA found that, in 2007, fame was "the number one value communicated to preteens on popular TV," confirming in later findings that fame was the number one goal for their future. A survey cited by *Teen Vogue* shows that over 30% of 14 to 18-year-olds admitted to thinking they are likely to be famous one day. Becoming a celebrity seems to be viewed as a career choice, and with a long list of "wildly successful" celebrities who dropped out of school at 15—including Virgin's Richard Branson, singer Aretha Franklin and cult film director Quentin Tarantino—it is perhaps unsurprising that long-term achievements like pursuing a path of education pale in comparison with instantaneous, TV-grade opportunities.

But it's not all bad news. Shira Gabriel, a psychologist at the University of Buffalo, told TIME that "Perhaps some people who

FAST FACT

Some celebrities who got their start on reality TV include Laverne Cox, Nicole "Snooki" Polizi, Jamie Chung, Cardi B, and, of course the Kardashians. This doesn't even include stars who first appeared on competition and talent reality shows.

don't feel good about themselves and are not able to get what they want out of a real relationship because of a fear of rejection can feel a connection with a celebrity and get something positive out of that." A parasocial relationship is, in a way, perhaps better than loneliness, and a way to cope with the pressures of everyday life. A study of Chinese students found that those who "worshipped" their teachers, family members or other "non-stars" had higher self-esteem and educational success, showing the positive side of having role models.

Why Does Celebrity Culture Matter?

Today, celebrity rules our world. Famous names and famous faces sell us products, push social change and tell us whom to vote for. Politics itself has become an exercise in showmanship. Ever since John F. Kennedy's youthful glow won him the 1960 run against Richard Nixon, the figure of the celebrity politician has become more ubiquitous. To win elections, not only did you have to be intelligent, competent and diligent; you had to look presidential as well.

You can see the mass appeal in the likes of Vladimir Putin's impressive public image campaign, or Narendra Modi's sweeping popularity or indeed Donald Trump's rise to power, which was made possible in large part by the persona created for him and popularized on *The Apprentice*.

While fame is not a new concept, its nature changed dramatically over the course of the 20th century. In the past, people were famous, or infamous, for being successful—the early Arctic explorers like Roald Amundsen and Ernest Shackleton, Amelia Earhart, Jeanne D'Arc, Galileo, Ernest Hemingway. Today, when someone like Paris Hilton or Kim Kardashian shoots to fame after releasing a sex tape, where footballers' wives and girlfriends are known for just that—being "WAGs"—we need to ask ourselves what value we assign to the people who dominate what is starting to feel like every aspect of our lives.

When The Beatles declared they were more popular than Jesus, were they aware of a cultural shift in public perception? After all, is Elvis ever less revered by the 20 million who have visited Graceland since it first opened in 1982 than Siddhartha Gautama, the historical Buddha?

In a culture where Grumpy Cat earns more than professional actors and sportsmen, we need to hold a mirror up to our social nature and try to understand this need to identify with someone, and to attempt to move past being trapped in what often feels like a cliquey, Mean Girls-style high-school cafeteria.

EVALUATING THE AUTHOR'S ARGUMENTS:

Viewpoint author Anna Pivovarchuk argues that celebrities used to achieve fame for accomplishments, but now people can achieve celebrity for much less. How can this have a negative impact on young people?

Facts About Celebrity Culture

Editor's note: These facts can be used in reports to add credibility when making important points or claims.

Museums Dedicated to Celebrites

- Madame Tussaud's Waxworks
- Graceland Museum (for Elvis Presley) in Memphis, TN
- The Arnold Schwarzenegger Museum in Thal, Austria
- The Britney Spears Exhibit in Kentwood, LA
- The Jackie Chan Museum in Shanghai, China
- The Stoogeum (for the 3 Stooges) in Ambler, PA

Common Quote About Fame

"In the future, everyone will be world-famous for 15 minutes," by Andy Warhol.

Some people say this is where the phrase "15 minutes of fame" came from.

Disorders Associated with Celebrity Obsession

- Beauty Dysmorphia: A constant compulsion or obsession with having to look perfect. At one time celebrities battled with this having to look perfect all the time. Now it is happening with non-celebrities as a result of social media intrusion into every-day lives.
- Celebrity Worship Syndrome: An obsessive-addictive disorder where a person becomes overly interested or obsessed with the details of the personal lives of celebrities.
- Erotomania: The sufferer has delusion that they are having a relationship with another person. This happens often with people thinking celebrities they see have this secret relationship with them.

3 Dimensions of Celebrity Worship Syndrome (CWS)

- Entertainment-Social: Certain individuals are attracted to celebrities because of the entertainment associated with fame. They then focus their attentions to finding other people like them to worship these celebrities.
- Intense Personal: Individuals that have intensive feelings about a celebrity.
- Borderline Pathological: Individuals that have uncontrollable behaviors and fantasies about a particular celebrity.

Top Ten Highest Paid Celebrities 2019

- Taylor Swift—$185 million
- Kylie Jenner—$170 million
- Kanye West—$150 million
- Lionel Messi—$127 million
- Ed Sheeran—$110 million
- Cristiano Ronaldo—$109 million
- NEYMAR—$105 million
- The Eagles—$100 million
- Dr. Phil—$95 million
- Canelo Alvarez—$94 million

Organizations to Contact

The editors have compiled the following list of organizations concerned with the issues debated in this book. The descriptions are derived from materials provided by the organizations. All have publications or information available for interested readers. The list was compiled on the date of publication of the present volume; the information provided here may change. Be aware that many organizations take several weeks or longer to respond to inquiries, so allow as much time as possible for the receipt of requested materials.

American Psychological Association (APA)
750 First Street NE
Washington, DC 20002-4242
(800) 374-2721
email: Use link on contact page.
website: www. apa.org/index
The American Psychological Association, the leading scientific association of psychology in the United States, has a wealth of information on its website. The APA offers insight into many important topics, but one, "Kids & the Media," is especially timely.

ANAD (National Association of Anorexia Nervosa and Associated Disorders)
220 N. Green Street
Chicago, IL 60607
(630) 577-1333
email: hello@anad.org
website: //anad.org/
The ANAD is a nonprofit organization started in 1976 which is dedicated to providing help for those suffering from eating disorders. This is important to the topic of celebrity culture because some people are so affected by saturation of media coverage of celebrities and their culture that they develop eating disorders and other associated psychological problems.

Consumer Affairs Online
297 Kingsbury Grade
Suite 1025, Mailbox 4470
Lake Tahoe, NV 89449-4470
(866) 773-0221
email: Use links on contact page.
website: www.consumeraffairs.com/
Consumer Affairs is an organization usually equated with online and print venues offering tips, advice, recommendations, and ratings that help consumers when purchasing various items. Consumer Affairs Online also offers family and parenting news including articles that analyze the effects of celebrity culture on individuals.

The Conversation
The Conversation Media Group, Level 1
715 Swanston St., Parkville, VIC, 3010
email: Use links on contact page.
website: www.theconversation.com/au
The Conversation is an independent news site dedicated to bringing high quality, trusted journalism to readers. The Conversation has special articles designed for "Curious Kids" and by using the search function, many articles can be accessed about celebrity culture.

Greater Good Science Center
University of California at Berkeley, MC 6070
Berkeley, CA 94720-6070
(510) 642-2490
email: Greater@berkeley.edu
website: www.greatergood.berkeley.edu
Greater Good Science Center Magazine takes scientific research and turns it into stories, tips, and tools to use and obtain a happier life. Use the articles, interactive quizzes, videos, and podcasts to help achieve a balanced, meaningful life.

Norman Lear Center
USC Annenberg School for Communication and Journalism
Los Angeles, CA, 90089-0281
(213) 821-1343
email: enter@usc.edu
website: www.learcenter.org
The Norman Lear Center is a nonpartisan public policy and research institute that studies the impact of entertainment in all its forms on the world. Use this site and inform yourself by watching videos, reading articles, visiting the blog, and checking out the extensive publications offered.

Psychology Today
115 E. 23rd Street, 9th Floor
New York, NY 10010
email: Use their "About Psychology Today" page.
website: www.psychologytoday.com/us
Psychology Today website maintains a robust catalog of articles related to the issues of celebrity culture. Use the search function to find information about celebrity worship syndrome and many other impactful topics.

UNICEF USA
125 Maiden Lane
New York, NY, 10038
(800) 367-5437
email: Use links on contact page.
website: www.unicefusa.org/
UNICEF USA is a charitable organization dedicated to providing humanitarian relief to those in need in times of emergency. Read about this agency's efforts, and also the many celebrities who actively support the work as UNICEF ambassadors and supporters.

For Further Reading

Books

Anderson, Judith. *Celebrity and Fame*. Mankato/MN: Amicus, 2011. Find out about how the media treats famous people around the globe. Read about the issues impacting celebrities including discrimination, privacy issues, paparazzi and continuous scrutiny by the media.

Caulfield, Timothy A. *Is Gywneth Paltrow Wrong About Everything?: How the Famous Sell Us Elixirs of Health, Beauty & Happiness*. Boston/MA: Beacon Press, 2015. Some celebrities are in the business of giving advice on many aspects in life. Why do people put faith in this advice? The author gives personal experience trying to break into celebrity culture by auditioning for *American Idol*.

Douglas, Susan J. Celebrity: *A History of Fame*. New York/NY: New York University Press, 2019. Celebrity was not always an overwhelming part of life. This book explores how technology has evolved and changed the abundance of celebrity culture.

Fahy, Declan. *The New Celebrity Scientists: Out of the Lab and Into the Limelight*. New York/NY: Rowman & Littlefield, 2015. Begins with a short history of scientific celebrities. Then read about modern scientific celebrities such as Stephen Hawking, Neil DeGrasse Tyson, Susan Greenfield and others.

Levy, Michael S. *Celebrity and Entertainment Obsession: Understanding Our Addiction*. Lanham/MD: Rowman & Littlefield, 2015. At one time celebrities gave the world something to be proud of, but not now. Levy explores this concept and how the public has an insatiable appetite for information about people in the entertainment business.

Marcus, Sharon. *The Drama of Celebrity*. Princeton/NJ: Princeton University Press, 2019. Read all about the topic of celebrities and celebrity culture. Who gets to be a star? What about the fans? Why are people so enamored with celebrities?

Projansky, Sarah. *Spectactular Girls: Media Fascination and Celebrity Culture*. New York: New York University Press, 2016. The book addresses two key themes within the greater discussion of girls: simultaneous adoration and disdain for girls and the pervasiveness of whiteness and heteronormativity.

Ross, Steven Joseph. *Hollywood Left and Right: How Movie Stars Shaped American Politics*. New York/NY: Oxford University Press, 2011. As the title suggests, read about the stars and how they have influenced America's political process. From the earliest stars up to recent influencers, get the whole story.

Turner, Graeme. *Understanding Celebrity*. Thousand Oaks, SAGE Publications, 2014. Examines the connection between the production and consumption of the manufactured persona of celebrity.

Walsh, Kenneth T. *Celebrity in Chief: A History of the Presidents and the Culture of Stardom*. Boulder/CO: Paradigm Publishers, 2015. All about the US presidents from Washington to Obama and how they have become stars. Also, information about the first ladies, and interesting details about pets, foods, sports, fashions, and more.

Warner, Helen. *Fashion on Television: Identity and Celebrity Culture*. London, England: Bloomsbury, 2014. This book provides a comprehensive critical examination of the intersection between fashion, television and celebrity culture.

Periodicals and Internet Sources

Cipriano, Andrea, "How the Media Abets 'Fame-Seeking' Mass Shooters," Crime Report, October 11, 2019. https://thecrimereport. org/2019/10/11/fame-seeking-mass-shooters-get-the-attention-they-want-study/.

Clausen, Christopher, "FDR's Hidden Handicap," *Wilson Quarterly*, Summer 2005. archive.wilsonquarterly.com/essays/fdrs-hidden-handicap.

Fletcher, Winston, "Why Are We So Fascinated by Fame?" *Guardian*, October 9, 2006. https://www.theguardian.com/commentis-free/2006/oct/09/whyarewesofascinatedbyfa.

Garber, Megan, "Harvey Weinstein and the Power of Celebrity Exceptionalism," *Atlantic*, October 13, 2017. https://www.theatlantic.com/

entertainment/archive/2017/10/harvey-weinstein-and-the-power-of-celebrity-exceptionalism/542880/

Gypsyy, Fotinoula, "10 Reasons Why Being Famous Isn't All that Great," Reel Rundown, May 23, 2016. https://reelrundown.com/celebrities/10-Reasons-Why-Being-Famous-Isnt-All-That-Great.

Healy, Melissa, "For Mass Shooters, Achieving Fame -- or Infamy -- is a Frequent Driver," *Los Angeles Times*, October 2, 2015. https://www.latimes.com/science/sciencenow/la-sci-sn-mass-shooters-fame-infamy-20151002-story.html.

Heflick, Nathan A., "Why Are We Obsessed with Celebrities?" *Psychology Today*, December 9, 2009. https://www.psychologytoday.com/us/blog/the-big-questions/200912/why-we-are-obsessed-celebrities.

Hess, Amanda, "When Instagram Killed the Tabloid Star," *New York Times*, November 24, 2019. https://www.nytimes.com/2019/11/24/arts/celebrity-instagram.html

Hinsliff, Gaby, "Harry and Meghan are Celebrities, but That Doesn't Mean They Owe Us Everything," *Guardian*, October 4, 2019. https://www.theguardian.com/commentisfree/2019/oct/04/prince-harry-meghan-privacy-tabloid-media.

Neary, Lynn, "What Oprah's Endorsement Means for Obama," NPR, December 9, 2007. https://www.npr.org/templates/story/story.php?storyId=17055698.

Nesvig, Kara, "15 Awesome Female Celebrities Who Support Great Causes," *Teen Vogue*, March 9, 2016. https://www.teenvogue.com/gallery/celebrities-who-support-great-causes.

Nicholson, Nigel, "The New Word on Gossip," *Psychology Today*, June 9, 2016. https://www.psychologytoday.com/us/articles/200105/the-new-word-gossip.

Notopoulos, Katie, "Teens Say Social Media Isn't As Bad For Them As You Might Think," BuzzFeed News, November 28, 2018. https://www.buzzfeednews.com/article/katienotopoulos/teens-gen-z-positive-on-social-media.

Orange, Erica, Jared Weiner, and Eshanthi Ranasinghe, "The Rise—and Fall?—or the Social Media Influencer," Medium, March 7, 2019. https://medium.com/positive-returns/the-rise-and-fall-of-the-social-media-influence-28ee82eabf5d

Price, Lydia, "The Great Fame Debate: 8 Stars on Why They Either Love or Hate Life in the Spotlight," *People*, December 8, 2016. https://people.com/celebrity/celebrities-who-love-or-hate-fame/

Pugachevsky, Julia, "27 Celebrities on Dealing with Depression and Bipolar Disorder," Buzzfeed, November 7, 2014. https://www.buzzfeed.com/juliapugachevsky/celebrities-on-dealing-with-depression-and-bipolar-disord.

Ranscombe, Sian, "Are Celebrities Encouraging Young People to Have Cosmetic Surgery?" *Telegraph*, March 4, 2016. https://www.telegraph.co.uk/beauty/body/cosmetic-procedures-are-on-the-rise---if-youre-considering-going/.

Rosenblum, Emma, "Fixated on Fame? You're Not Alone, A Look at the Growing Obsession with Being a Star," *Teen Vogue*, November 19, 2013. https://www.teenvogue.com/story/celebrity-fame-obsession.

Rumble, Taylor-Dior, "Mid-Term Elections 2018: Do Celebrities Really Influence Voters?" BBC, November 7, 2018. https://www.bbc.com/news/entertainment-arts-46123964.

Schildkraut, Jaclyn, "The Media Should Stop Making School Shooters Famous," Vox, March 31, 2018. https://www.vox.com/the-big-idea/2018/2/22/17041382/school-shooting-media-coverage-perpetrator-parkland

Schulten, Katherine, "Why Does Celebrity Gossip Interest Us So Much? *New York Times*, September 22, 2016. https://www.nytimes.com/2016/09/22/learning/why-does-celebrity-gossip-interest-us-so-much.html.

Shankel, Jason, "The Cosmos is All That is, Or Ever Was, or Ever Will Be," GIZMODO, March 10, 2014. https://io9.gizmodo.com/the-cosmos-is-all-that-is-or-ever-was-or-ever-will-b-1540197550.

Shapiro, Ben, "America Needs to Stop Treating Celebrities Like Politicians," *Newsweek*, January 17, 2020. https://www.newsweek.com/ben-shapiro-america-needs-stop-treating-celebrities-politicians-opinion-964370

Weaver, Nicole, "7 of the Most Charitable Celebrities in Hollywood," Showbiz CheatSheet, August 29, 2017. https://www.cheatsheet.com/entertainment/most-charitable-celebrities-hollywood.html/.

Websites

AMC Filmsite (www.filmsite.org/100greatfilmstars.html)
Find the top one hundred film stars of all time, divided into fifty actors and fifty actresses. Information includes each stars best movies.

Oprah Winfrey Endorses Barack Obama
(www.oprah.com/world/why-oprah-cndorsed-barack-obama)
Listen to Oprah Winfrey talk about how she knew that Barack Obama would one day run for president. Also, how she helped by publicly using her celebrity influence to get others to back Obama for president.

***TIME*—100 Most Significant Figures in History**
(ideas.time.com/2013/12/10/whos-biggest-the-100-most
-significant-figures-in-history/)
Look at the list of history's one hundred most important people as determine by *TIME* magazine.

Index

Picture Credits

Cover Paul Bradbury/OJO Images/Getty Images; p. 10 moodboard/ Getty Images; p. 13 Steve Parsons/PA Images/Getty Images; p. 18 TheVisualsYouNeed/Shutterstock.com; p. 22 John Lamparski/Getty Images; p. 28 Neilson Barnard/Getty Images; pp. 33, 85 Getty Images; p. 38 Corbis Historical/Getty Images; p. 43 Hero Images/ Getty Images; p. 46 Kevin Mazur/WireImage/Getty Images; p. 51 Tim Hall/Cultura/Getty Images; p. 57 Joe Sohm/Visions of America/ Universal Images Group/Getty Images; p. 63 PG/Bauer-Griffin/GC Images/Getty Images; p. 68 ViChizh/Shutterstock.com; p. 72 stock-aboo/Shutterstock.com; p. 75 Klaus Vedfelt/DigitalVision/Getty Images; p. 80 Gareth Cattermole/Getty Images; p. 85 Getty Images; p. 90 Sylvain Lefevre/Getty Images; p. 95 Jessica McGowan/Getty Images; p. 101 OpturaDesign/Shutterstock.com.